THE CUNARD LINE

THE CUNARD LINE

A Pictorial History 1840-1990

by
Peter W. Woolley and Terry Moore

Foreword by
Capt. R.A. Woodall, R.D.*, R.N.R.

Ship Pictorial Publications
1990

This book is dedicated to the memory of the late John Brown (1941-1988), Ex-Cunarder and River Mersey Pilot.

"The first to say good-morrow, the last to say good-bye"
Liverpool Pilot Service

First published in 1990 by Ship Pictorial Publications
3 College Close, Coltishall, Norfolk NR12 7DT.

© Copyright 1990 Ship Pictorial Publications

ISBN 0 9516038 0 9

Typeset, printed and bound by Manchester Free Press, Paragon Mill, Jersey Street, Manchester M4 6FP.

CONTENTS

FOREWORD
by
Captain R.A. Woodall, R.D.*, R.N.R.
Master of the *Queen Elizabeth 2*

Little did I think in 1946 when I moved from my birthplace London to the great port of Liverpool, that I would be privileged and honoured to write a foreword to a book on Cunard Line.

Always having a hankering after the sea, this became a reality in 1950 when I joined my first ship, the Cunard cargo liner *Arabia,* in Huskisson dock, Liverpool to start my career with Cunard. Starting as a very wet-behind-the-ears apprentice it was always my ambition to sail in the great liners, having seen pictures of them in books such as this. I never then realised my ambition would culminate in being in command of *Queen Elizabeth 2,* but never the less very proud to be so.

In the intervening years there have been many changes in the face of ocean going passenger ships. From the heyday of the Atlantic ferry service, to today where the modern equivalent of these fine ships pursue a far more leisurely pace, but equally important role, in that of cruising. Cruising all over the world, and bringing the taste of sea travel to millions of people, with *Queen Elizabeth 2* maintaining the links with the past with her summer sailings across the Atlantic.

It is fitting that this book should depict Cunard liners of the past and present in this year 1990, the 150th anniversary of the first sailing of the Cunard's *Britannia* from the port of Liverpool in 1840.

I hope it will evoke memories for those who have sailed with this great company, and perhaps fire the imagination and ambition of youngsters who will sail with Cunard in the future.

My thanks to Peter Woolley and Terry Moore for another chapter in the great history of Cunard.

ix

A SHORT HISTORY OF THE CUNARD LINE

1840 British & North American Royal Mail Steam Packet Company
1878 Cunard Steam Ship Company Limited
1934 Cunard-White Star Limited
1949 Cunard Steam Ship Company Limited
1962 Cunard Line Limited

Nova Scotia was the birthplace of the man whose name later became synonymous with one of the great passenger liner companies of the North Atlantic.

Samuel Cunard was born at Halifax, Nova Scotia, on the 21st November 1787 and became one of the leading figures in the affairs of the city and as a business man, had a financial interest in shipping, one of which was the *Royal William,* the first steam-driven ship to cross the Atlantic from Canada in 1833.

The accepted means of crossing in those days was by sailing ship, the length of the passage being entirely dependent upon the weather and a duration of five to six weeks from London to New York was not uncommon. Steam-ships were, however, beginning to appear in the form of paddle-steamers, credit for the first such crossing going to the American *Savannah* in 1819 for a voyage from Savannah to Liverpool, then on to St. Petersburg (Leningrad) and subsequently returning to her home port at the end of November of that year.

Various other steamers went across from time to time but their primitive engines and boilers were in the main unreliable and costly to run, so that most together with companies owning them did not last too long. They all carried sails which could be usefully employed to assist when the wind was favourable or in the event of an engine breakdown. Nevertheless, the passage times were considerably less than those of the sailing packets, so much so that the British Admiralty invited tenders for the carriage of mail between England and North America by steam-ship in 1838. They had been particularly impressed by the successful transatlantic voyages of two paddle-steamers, the *Sirius* and *Great Western* earlier in the year with crossing times of under twenty days.

To secure a mail contract could be a very lucrative undertaking, for the company concerned would receive a considerable subsidy for the guaranteed frequency of sailings agreed with the Admiralty. The prestige involved would also attract the public to sail with the company whose ships were entrusted with the country's mail. But there were few companies and no ships existed that could carry out the frequency of service required. They had to be built.

Fired with enthusiasm for the project, Samuel Cunard then aged 51, sailed to England in January 1839 to personally offer his tender. Negotiations between himself, together with his shipbuilder Robert Napier and the Admiralty followed, culminating in a contract being signed for the provision of four steamers of 1,340 tons approximately to permit a sailing every two weeks with a monthly sailing between November and February inclusive for a subsidy of £56,000 per year from Liverpool to Halifax and Boston.

To help pay for the ships, Samuel Cunard approached three business men with shipping interests in Glasgow, George Burns, James Donaldson and David MacIver and together founded The British and North American Royal Mail Steam Packet Co. in 1840, popularly known from the beginning as the Cunard Line.

The first ship of the quartette, the *Britannia,* a wooden paddle-steamer left Liverpool on the 4th July 1840, with Samuel Cunard as a passenger, arriving in Halifax 12 days later, then on to Boston arriving 14 days 8 hours after leaving Liverpool. Homewards she arrived back in Liverpool 10 days after leaving Halifax. The second of the four, the *Acadia,* took slightly less time to reach Halifax, having left Liverpool on the 4th August 1840; she arrived in 11 days 4 hours. The remaining two ships, the *Caledonia* and *Columbia* followed on their maiden voyages the same year.

Although the service was being successfully operated, once again through lack of experience in the management of steam-ships, it was found that running costs were high and not being covered by charges and the subsidy. In the spring of 1841, the partners put their view forward to the Admiralty that they may have to terminate the service. After deliberation lasting until September, the Admiralty increased the subsidy to £81,000 per annum provided a fifth ship was constructed. Slightly larger than her predecessors, taking 120 passengers instead of 115 and about 100 tons more coal, the *Hibernia* was launched on the 8th September 1842.

From the start they vied not only with each other but also with ships of rival companies to obtain fast times. But although a new mail contract worth £156,000 per year for sailing via Halifax to Boston and New York, was entered into during 1847, competition was growing. The American Collins Line began operating in 1850 with ships both larger and more luxurious than any of Cunard's and by 1851 were crossing in half a day less, and the following year were carrying double the passengers of Cunard. During 1851 Cunard began operating to the Mediterranean, a trade that was eventually to become an important part of their business.

Sir Samuel Cunard died on 28th April 1865, having been knighted in 1859, and in 1869 the Company lost the Blue Riband to the Inman Line having held it for thirteen years, but worse was to follow for in 1871 the White Star Line, which had only been founded in 1869, brought out a class of liners for the Liverpool to New York route with compound engines and passenger accommodation very much superior to that of Cunard and eventually took the record for both Eastbound and Westbound crossings. Cunard did all it could to modernise its fleet but in order to pay for new-buildings more money was required than it was capable of raising. A new company, the Cunard Steam Ship Co. Ltd. was formed in 1878 to attract investment which enabled a new-building programme to be put in motion, though the Eastbound record was not recaptured until 1884 by the *Oregon* and the Westbound by the *Etruria* in 1885.

From this time the fortunes of the Company improved remarkably and it was able to construct express liners of ever increasing size to counter the challenges from other companies both British and foreign until the outbreak of the First World War. This rivalry brought improvements to the design of the ships themselves. Cunard's first steel hulled liner was the *Servia* of 1881 which also had electric-light in the passenger accommodation. Sails were discarded in 1893 with the *Campania* and *Lucania,* both of which had twin screws, again a first for Cunard. In 1905 came the *Carmania,* the first Cunarder with turbines and three screws.

Two large liners, the *Lusitania* and *Mauretania* at just under 32,000 g.r.t. had their maiden voyages in 1907, the *Lusitania* regaining the record from Germany in 1907 before finally losing it to the *Mauretania* which held it for the next twenty years.

Size also brought opulent luxury for the passengers, at least for those who could afford it; the wealthy were well catered for with magnificent food, wines and public rooms which in some cases bordered on the ostentatious. Even the non-travelling public became captivated by the stories in their newspapers of high living and extravagance by the wealthy and famous. Besides reading of the lavishness on board these majestic ships, they were made aware of the continuous struggle for recognition for having the fastest, largest, the most luxurious and the most powerful, so that in 1911, in answer to the introduction of the White Star's 45,324 g.r.t. *Olympic* the first of three large liners, the other two being the *Titanic* of 1912 and the *Britannic* of 1915, Cunard replied with the 45,647 g.r.t. *Aquitania,* sailing on her maiden voyage on the 30th May 1914. Though not intended to be a record breaker, her tonnage was half as much again as that of the *Lusitania* and *Mauretania* and her accommodation was magnificent.

Entry into the Canadian trade was made in 1911 with the acquisition of the Canadian business of the Thomson Line and their three ships, followed in 1912 by the Anchor Line of Glasgow.

During the First World War Cunard lost twenty ships from the fleet due to enemy action including the *Lusitania* which was torpedoed in May 1915 with heavy loss of life. The White Star had already lost the *Titanic* in the well-publicised disaster of 1912 and the *Britannic* had been mined and sunk in November 1916 while serving as a hospital ship. After the Armistice all liner companies were hard-pressed to run a service with their depleted fleets. Liners that had worked hard either on Government employment or normal trading during hostilities were in need of refits. Cunard brought the ex-German *Imperator* 52,226 g.r.t. from the British Shipping Controller in 1921 renaming her *Berengaria,* having managed her since 1919. She was sent for reconditioning together with the *Aquitania* and *Mauretania* and it was not until 1922 that the full service was restored. The post-war rebuilding programme of eleven ships was completed in 1925.

In July 1929, the *Bremen* 51,656 g.r.t. of the Norddeutscher Lloyd took the Blue Riband from the *Mauretania* on her maiden voyage. For some time the Company had been considering replacement for some of the older express liners and an order was placed with John Brown, Clydebank in 1930 for a very large liner, known at the time by her yard number of "534", whose keel was laid on the 27th December 1930. The Great Depression halted work on her after twelve months, being resumed in April 1934 with Government financial assistance providing a sister-ship was built and that Cunard and the White Star Line amalgamated to become the Cunard-White Star Line Ltd. The merger took effect from February 1934 involving only the transatlantic ships of both Companies, which still retained their original funnel colours.

The French Line's *Normandie* 79,280 g.r.t. took the Blue Riband from the *Bremen* on her maiden voyage in 1935, which was in turn regained for Cunard by the *Queen Mary* 80,774 g.r.t. which was the name given to number "534". Although she came into service in May 1936 it was not until August 1936 that she took the record from the *Normandie*.

A new *Mauretania* was completed by Cammell Laird, Birkenhead early in 1939. Of 35,739 g.r.t. she was the first liner to be ordered for the new company, Cunard-White Star Ltd. and at that time was the largest liner built in England.

Work started on the *Queen Mary's* consort, rather than a sister-ship, by Clydebank in December 1936 but before completion the Second World War had intervened and changed the course of history.

The *Queen Mary* crossed the Atlantic to be laid up with the *Mauretania* and her friendly rival, the *Normandie,* being joined by the hurriedly completed *Queen Elizabeth* 83,673 g.r.t. on the 7th March 1940. Both the "Queens" were required as troop ships, sailing to Sydney, Australia via Singapore for conversion, the *Queen Mary* leaving New York in March and the *Queen Elizabeth* in November 1940.

The Second World War saw the loss of six ships sunk plus another four which were purchased by the Admiralty and converted into heavy repair ships for the Navy.

Rebuilding began in 1946 not only of ships but of the trade routes themselves. The Canadian "A" Class was down to one, the *Ascania,* and three survivors of the five 20,000 ton ships, all of which were over 20 years old.

Whilst the fleet reconstruction was progressing the Cunard Steam-Ship Co. took over its wholly owned subsidiary, Cunard-White Star Ltd. in 1947, leading to its disappearance at the end of 1949, the only evidence remaining of its existence being the *Britannic* of 1930 and *Georgic* of 1932 with their buff funnels.

Also in 1949, a new *Caronia* 34,183 g.r.t. made her appearance, leaving Southampton on 4th January for her maiden voyage, and designed primarily for the American market, sailing on the North Atlantic in the summer and cruising from New York at other times. Having just one mast and funnel, her decks were clear of all unnecessary obstructions, and her hull and superstructure were painted three shades of green.

Four 22,000 g.r.t. ships were constructed during the period 1954-57 for the Canadian service, and by 1960 the Company was operating ten excellent liners but air travel was by now taking away passengers at an alarming rate, while making operating costs rose inexorably. To offset this, some ships were sold but by 1965 the Canadian service was no longer able to sustain the four liners built for it. The *Saxonia* and *Ivernia* were therefore withdrawn and modified for cruising, the two other sisters remaining on the Canadian route until sold out of the fleet in 1968 for further trading. In the meantime due to the decline, the pre-war *Mauretania* was broken up in 1965.

A subsidiary company, Cunard Line Ltd. was formed on 1st August 1962 to take over the management of the fleet of the Cunard Steam-Ship Company Ltd., of all the chartered ships operated by them and of all their offices and branches.

The decline in passenger traffic crossing the Atlantic by sea was by now unstoppable and 1967 saw the *Queen Mary* sold followed by the *Queen Elizabeth* in 1968.

The 2nd May 1969 was the date of the maiden voyage of the *Queen Elizabeth 2* of 65,863 g.r.t. from Southampton and Havre to New York. Again, she had been designed for cruising world-wide as well as liner voyages on the North Atlantic. She was at first beset with engine and boiler troubles which once cured enabled her to become a highly regarded cruise liner of international standing. She was requisitioned for the Falklands War in May 1982 returning to Cunard and a much needed refit at the end of hostilities. Her steam turbines were removed in 1986 to be replaced by diesel electric propulsion in order to save considerably in fuel costs; a reduction of 250 tons per day being achieved. Variable pitch propellers were also fitted during this £100 million refit at Bremerhaven, Germany.

1971 brought a new twist in the fortunes of the Company, when Trafalgar House Investments made a successful bid for the shares of Cunard and during the same year the *Cunard Adventurer* and the year following *Cunard Ambassador*, the last two ships ordered by Cunard Steam-Ship Co. before being taken over, came into service both entirely for cruising.

The appearance of the Company had now completely changed from the days when it was a household name in the North Atlantic liner trade with ships competing for the Blue Riband. Henceforth, passenger ships were built exclusively for cruising. Diversification had taken place however, for in 1967 the cargo division took a share in Atlantic Container Line Ltd., followed in 1968 by the formation of Cunard-Brocklebank Ltd., for which an order was placed for eight bulk carriers, which once delivered only remained in the fleet for some five years before being sold for further trading. Today after 150 years, however, it is still the passenger trade, and above all *Queen Elizabeth 2* that maintains the Cunard name in the public eye.

SAMUEL CUNARD, 1787-1865

Samuel Cunard was born on 21st November 1787 in Halifax, Nova Scotia. He joined his father's shipping company in 1804 and in 1819, when his father retired, Samuel and his brothers took over control of the company. In 1827 his wife died and with the help of his mother-in-law, he brought up nine children. Cunard worked harder than ever and by 1837 he owned forty ships. During a visit to England, he was so impressed with the performance of the 'Rocket', that he decided that the future of transatlantic travel must be by steamships. At first his ideas were not supported, but following an advertisement for tenders for steamships to carry mails across the Atlantic, he raised sufficient capital, and after many problems, he was awarded the contract by the British Government.

Samuel Cunard joined up with three Scottish businessmen, George Burns, James Donaldson and David MacIver, and between them formed the British and North American Royal Mail Steam Packet Company, later to be known as the Cunard Steam Ship Company. Four ships were ordered and the first ship, the *Britannia,* was completed in 1840. At the age of 53, Cunard had realised his dream and the beginning of a great shipping company. In March 1859, in recognition of his pioneering work on the transatlantic route and helping with the Crimean War effort, he was honoured with a knighthood at the age of 72. Cunard retired in 1863 and died on 28th April 1865.

BRITANNIA, 1840-1849

Paddle-steamer. Wooden hull. Built by Robert Duncan & Co., Greenock, Scotland. Tonnage: 1,139 g.r.t.; 619 net. 207' x 34.2' x 24.4'. 740 i.h.p. Service speed 9 kts. 115 passengers. Her maiden voyage commenced on 4th July 1840 from Liverpool to Halifax (Nova Scotia) and Boston; the voyage lasting 12 days, 10 hours to Halifax and a further 46 hours to Boston. The *Britannia* took the eastbound record of the Blue Riband in August 1840 with a time of ten days exactly, retaining the record until June 1842. In February 1844, the *Britannia* became trapped in Boston Harbour when the sea froze over. Her wooden hull became endangered by the ice and the merchants of Boston organised a fund to pay for a team of men to cut a seven-mile long channel to free the ship. (The above picture shows the *Britannia* making its way out of the channel.) Sold in 1849 to the North German Confederate Navy, converted to a frigate and renamed *Barbarossa*. Sunk in 1880 when acting as a target ship.

DAMASCUS, 1856-1865

Single screw steamer. Iron hull. Built in 1856 by William Denny & Bros., Dumbarton. 1,214 g.r.t. 253.5′ x 32′ x 22.1′. 2 cylinders, 2 boilers, 5 furnaces. Passengers: 40 first class and 300 third class. She was laid down as the *St George* for D.R. Macgregor, Leith. Acquired by Cunard for Mediterranean service and renamed *Damascus*. 1865 — Purchased by Allan Line retaining the same name. 1870 — Lengthened, refitted and renamed *Corinthian*. 1881 — Sold to Italian owners. 1912 — Scrapped after having had several further Italian and Turkish owners and name changes.

SCOTIA, 1862-1878

Paddle-steamer. Iron hull. Built in 1862 by Robert Napier & Sons, Glasgow. 3,871 g.r.t, 2,125 net. 397′ o.a. 379.3′ b.p. x 47.6′ x 30.5′. 14 knots service speed. 4,900 i.h.p. Passengers: 275 cabin class and 300 second class. 440 crew. Last of Cunard's transatlantic paddle-steamers. The *Scotia* was completed with three masts but eventually reduced to two before her first voyage. Except for the *Great Eastern,* she was the largest ship afloat. Her maiden voyage commenced on 10th May 1862 from Liverpool to New York under the command of Capt. C.H. Judkins. Between July 1866 and May 1872 she held the westbound record for the Blue Riband with a time of 8 days, 4 hours and 35 minutes (av. spd. 14.51 kts.), and between December 1863 and July 1869, the eastbound record with a time of 8 days and 3 hours (av. spd. 14.02 kts). In 1878 she was sold to the Telegraph Construction and Maintenance Company and converted to a cable layer by Laird Bros. On the 11th March, 1904, she was wrecked on Catalan Bank, Guam.

RUSSIA, 1867-1881

Single screw steamer. Iron hull. Built in 1867 by J. & G. Thomson & Co. Glasgow. 2,959 g.r.t.,
1,400 net. 358′ x 42.6′ x 28′. 14 knots service speed. 3,100 i.h.p. Passengers: 430 saloon class.
The last Cunarder to be built with a clipper bow.

Her maiden voyage commenced on 15th June 1867 from Liverpool to New York. She held the
eastbound record for the Blue Riband from July 1867 to December 1869 with a time of 8 days
and 30 minutes (av. spd. 14.19 kts), having taken the record from the *Scotia*. Her last voyage was
on 2nd November 1878 from New York and in 1881 she was sold to the Red Star Line and renamed
the *Waesland*. 5th March, 1902 — Sunk off Anglesey after a collision with a British steamer.

SERVIA, 1881-1902

Single screw steamer. Steel hull. Built in 1881 by J. & G. Thomson & Co., Glasgow. 7,391 g.r.t., 3,971 net. 515′ x 52.3′ x 39.9′. 16 kts service speed. Passengers: 480 first class with 202 staterooms, 500 third class. 252 crew of which 105 were stewards. The first Cunarder to be built of steel and the first steamship in the world to be lit throughout by electricity.

At the time, the *Servia* was the largest ship afloat after the *Great Eastern* and the first express passenger ship to rely entirely on revenue from the lucrative passenger trade across the North Atlantic. Later she was converted to an armed merchant cruiser with ten guns, and during the Boer War used as a transport ship for the Government at a cost of 21 shillings (£1.05) per ton per month. Her final voyage from New York commenced on 17th September 1901 and she was sold to Thomas Ward in 1902 to be broken up at Preston, Lancashire.

AURANIA, 1883-1905

Single screw steamer. Steel hull. Built in 1883 by J. & G. Thomson & Co., Glasgow. 7,268 g.r.t., 4,030 net. 470' x 57.3' x 37.5'. 17 knots service speed. 9,900 i.h.p. Passengers: 500 first class with 213 staterooms, 700 third class. 275 crew.

The *Aurania* was never a popular ship with her passengers as she rolled badly due to her narrow beam. Her maiden voyage from Liverpool to New York commenced on 23rd June 1883. Later, in 1899, during the Boer War, she became transport ship no.20. In 1905, the *Aurania* was sold for £18,450 and broken up in Italy. The two illustrations show the ship illustrated from part of the front cover of an early menu card, and the front cover of an 1887 concert programme held in aid of the Liverpool Seamen's orphanage and Home for Destitute Children of Seamen, Staten Island, N.Y.

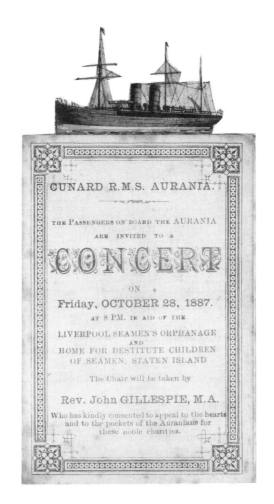

CUNARD R.M.S. AURANIA.

THE PASSENGERS ON BOARD THE AURANIA ARE INVITED TO A

CONCERT

ON

Friday, OCTOBER 28, 1887.

AT 8 P.M. IN AID OF THE

LIVERPOOL SEAMEN'S ORPHANAGE AND HOME FOR DESTITUTE CHILDREN OF SEAMEN, STATEN ISLAND

The Chair will be taken by

Rev. John GILLESPIE, M.A.

Who has kindly consented to appeal to the hearts and to the pockets of the Auranians for these noble charities.

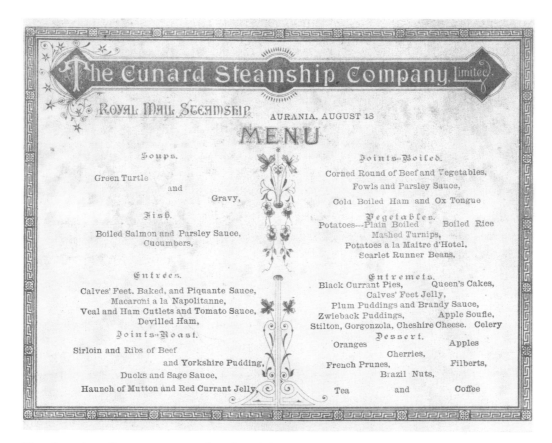

The Cunard Steamship Company, Limited

ROYAL MAIL STEAMSHIP
AURANIA, AUGUST 13
MENU

Soups.

Green Turtle

and

Gravy,

Fish.

Boiled Salmon and Parsley Sauce,
Cucumbers,

Entrées.

Calves' Feet, Baked, and Piquante Sauce,
Macaroni a la Napolitanne,
Veal and Ham Cutlets and Tomato Sauce,
Devilled Ham,

Joints–Roast.

Sirloin and Ribs of Beef
and Yorkshire Pudding,
Ducks and Sage Sauce,
Haunch of Mutton and Red Currant Jelly,

Joints–Boiled.

Corned Round of Beef and Vegetables,
Fowls and Parsley Sauce,
Cold Boiled Ham and Ox Tongue

Vegetables.

Potatoes---Plain Boiled   Boiled Rice
Mashed Turnips,
Potatoes a la Maitre d'Hotel,
Scarlet Runner Beans,

Entremets.

Black Currant Pies,   Queen's Cakes,
Calves' Feet Jelly,
Plum Puddings and Brandy Sauce,
Zwieback Puddings,   Apple Soufle,
Stilton, Gorgonzola, Cheshire Cheese. Celery

Dessert.

Oranges   Apples
Cherries,
French Prunes,   Filberts,
Brazil Nuts,

Tea   and   Coffee

The above is a dinner menu served on board the *Aurania* during a voyage in 1883. The front of the menu shows a drawing of the *Aurania* and a list of leading British hotels. The back of the menu carries a list of various advertisements and a list of the Cunard fleet for the Atlantic, Mediterranean and Le Havre services.

ETRURIA, 1884-1909

Single screw steamer. Steel hull. Built in 1884 by John Elder & Co., Fairfield, Glasgow. 8,128 g.r.t., 3,690 net. 500′ x 57.3′ x 39.0′. Service speed 19.5 kts. 14,500 i.h.p. Passengers: 550 first class and 800 third class. Sister-ship to the *Umbria* (8,120 g.r.t.) built the same year. The first Cunarders to have refrigeration machinery and the largest ship of the Cunard fleet at the time. The last Cunarders to have auxiliary sail.

The *Etruria* commenced her maiden voyage on 25th April 1885 from Liverpool to New York. Prior to the voyage, during the Russian scare, she was prepared and fitted out as an armed merchant cruiser. She held the westbound record for the Blue Riband between May 1888 and May 1889 with a time of 6 days, one hour and 55 minutes (average speed — 19.57 kts); and the eastbound record between March 1887 and May 1889 with a time of 6 days, 4 hours and 36 minutes (average speed — 19.45 kts). Fitted with wireless in 1901. Sold for £16,750 in 1909 and broken up at Preston, Lancashire.

9

CAMPANIA, 1893-1914
Twin screw steamer. Steel hull. Built
in 1893 by the Fairfield Shipbuilding
and Engineering Co., Glasgow.
12,950 g.r.t., 4,974 net. 620′ o.a. 600′
b.p. x 65.3′ x 40.6′. Service speed
21kts. Passengers: 526 first class, 280
second class and 1,000 steerage class.
415 crew. The first twin screw
Cunarder, and the first ship to have
'en suite' rooms and built
specifically with single berth cabins.
Sister-ship to *Lucania*.

S. S. "Campania" & Landing Stage, Liverpool

CAMPANIA, 1893-1914

The *Campania* commenced her maiden voyage on 22nd April 1893 from Liverpool to New York. Until 1897, the *Lucania* and the *Campania* were the largest ships in the world. She broke the westbound record for the Blue Riband in August 1894 in a time of 5 days 9 hours and 29 minutes (av. spd. 21.49 kts), and held the eastbound record between May 1893 and May 1894 in a time of 5 days 17 hours and 27 minutes (av. spd. 21.09 kts). Sold to the Admiralty in November 1914 and converted to a seaplane carrier by Cammell Laird, Birkenhead, and renamed H.M.S. *Campania*. On 5th November 1918 she collided with the battleship H.M.S. *Revenge* in the Firth of Forth and sank. All the crew were saved.

**PASSENGER LOG-BOOK,
R.M.S. CAMPANIA**
Illustrating the front cover of the
Cunard passenger log-book, issued to
passengers who sailed on the
Campania in 1893. The 96-page
booklet provided a history of Cunard,
a fleet list, a detailed description of
the liner, and many fascinating
advertisements.

THE CUNARD LINE.

FLEET OF STEAMSHIPS—OCEAN SERVICE.

CAMPANIA.	SCYTHIA.	KEDAR.
LUCANIA.	PAVONIA.	MOROCCO.
UMBRIA.	CEPHALONIA.	PALMYRA.
ETRURIA.	CATALONIA.	TARIFA.
AURANIA.	SAMARIA.	ALEPPO.
SERVIA.	ATLAS.	TRINIDAD.
GALLIA.	MARATHON.	CHERBOURG.
BOTHNIA.	SARAGOSSA.	BRITISH QUEEN.

The Cunard Steam Ship Company, Ltd.

Directors, Principal Officers, Principal Establishments, &c.

DIRECTORS.

Sir JOHN BURNS, Bart., *Chairman of the Board.*
DAVID JARDINE, *Chairman of Executive Committee.*
WILFRID A. BEVAN.   Sir WM. BOWER FORWOOD.
WILLIAM CUNARD.   JOHN WILLIAMSON.

PRINCIPAL OFFICERS—LIVERPOOL.

THOMAS BOUMPHREY, *General Manager.*
ALBERT P. MOORHOUSE, *Secretary.*
Commander WM. WATSON, R.N.R., *General Superintendent.*
JAMES BAIN, R.N.R., *Superintendent Engineer.*

PRINCIPAL ESTABLISHMENTS.

Great Britain & Ireland.

Liverpool—8 Water St. (Head Office)
      ,,   1 Rumford Street.
London { Palmerston Buildings, Bishopsgate St., E.C.
      ,,   13 Pall Mall, S.W.
Glasgow—30 Jamaica Street.
Manchester—13 Brazenose Street.
Queenstown—3 Scott's Square.
Belfast—49 Queen's Square.

Abroad—Agents.

New York—Vernon H. Brown & Co., 4 Bowling Green.
Boston—Alex. Martin, 99 State St.
Chicago—F. G. Whiting, 131 Randolph Street.
Havre—James Winning, 21 Quai d'Orleans.
Paris—Antoni Drouard, 38 Avenue de l'Opera.

———:o:———

Sailings from Liverpool for New York every Saturday and alternate Tuesday; and for Boston every Thursday.
Sailings from New York every Saturday and alternate Tuesday; and from Boston every Saturday.

17

PAGE FROM LOG-BOOK — R.M.S. CAMPANIA, 1893
Details of the company, ships in service and agents.

THE CUNARD LINE.

ESTABLISHED 1840.

These Steamers have, for over Fifty Years, an unequalled record for the safety and comfort of their passengers, and take specified tracks on the Outward and Homeward Voyages, as adopted by all the leading Companies.

NEW YORK SATURDAY
MAIL SERVICE.

Sailing from New York and Liverpool every Saturday calling at Queenstown.

"Campania"	12,950 tons	Capt. HAINS, R.N.R.
"Lucania"	12,950 tons	Capt. H. McKAY, R.N.R.
"Etruria"	8,119 tons	Capt. WALKER, R.N.R.
"Umbria,'	8,127 tons	Capt. DUTTON.

FORTNIGHTLY TUESDAY SERVICE.

"Aurania"	7,268 tons	Capt. A. McKAY.
"Servia"	7,391 tons	
"Gallia"	4,808 tons	Capt. FERGUSSON.

SALOON RATES.

Single Tickets from $60 to $175 or £12 to £35.
Return Tickets from $120 to $315 or £22 to £63.

According to the season of the year, the location of the room, and the Steamer chosen. Children between Two and Twelve, Half Fare.

SECOND CABIN RATES.

Single Tickets from $40 to $60 or £8 to £12.
Return Tickets from $75 to $110 or £15 to £22.

According to the season of the year, the location of the room, and the Steamer chosen. Children between Two and Twelve, Half Fare.
Summer Season begins on the 16th April and ends 15th October.
Winter Season begins on the 16th October and ends 15th April.

WEEKLY BOSTON SERVICE.

From Liverpool on Thursdays and Boston on Saturdays, calling at Queenstown.

"Cephalonia"	5,517 tons	Capt. SECCOMBE.
"Pavonia"	5,587 tons	Capt. WATT.
"Catalonia"	4,841 tons	Capt. ATKIN.
"Bothnia"	4,535 tons	Capt. THOMAS.
"Scythia"	4,557 tons	Capt. HEWITSON.

SALOON RATES.

Single Tickets from $60 to $175 or £12 to £35.
Return Tickets from $120 to $315 or £22 to £63.

According to the season of the year, and the location of the room.
Children between Two and Twelve, Half Fare.

SECOND CABIN RATES.

Single Tickets from $35 to $50 or £7 to £10.
Return Tickets from $70 to $95 or £13 to £19.

Summer Season begins on the 16th of April and ends 15th October.
Winter Season begins on the 16th October and ends 15th April.

STEERAGE RATES.—From $25 or 5 Guineas.

18

PAGE FROM LOG-BOOK — R.M.S. CAMPANIA, 1893
Details of sailings and various rates.

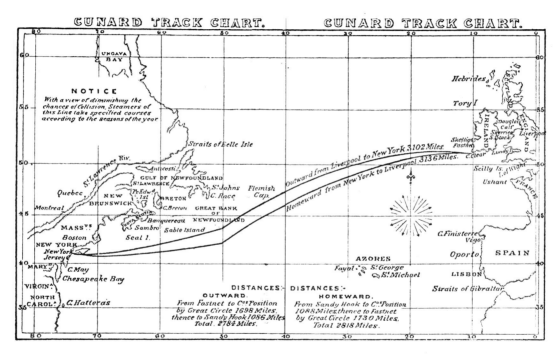

PAGE FROM LOG-BOOK — R.M.S CAMPANIA, 1893

Showing the Cunard route from Liverpool to New York — 3102 nautical miles, and New York to Liverpool — 3136 nautical miles. Notice the space at the bottom of the page for autographs.

CUNARD LINE POSTER

Showing the *Lucania* at the Liverpool landing-stage, and the interior of Riverside Station, Liverpool (see pages 43-44). Passengers can be seen boarding the Cunard Special, hauled by a Webb "Jumbo" class 2-4-0 owned by the London and North Western Railway Company. The journey to London Euston took 3 hours 50 minutes.

LUCANIA, 1893-1909

Twin screw steamer. Steel hull. Built in 1893 by Fairfield Shipbuilding and Engineering Company, Glasgow. Tonnage and dimensions identical to *Campania*.

The *Lucania* held the westbound record for the Blue Riband from October 1893 to August 1894 with a time of 5 days, 13 hours and 45 minutes (av. spd 20.75 kts) and breaking the record again in August 1894, September 1894 and October 1894 with her best time recorded at 5 days, 7 hours, 23 minutes. She held the eastbound record between May 1894 and November 1897 with a time of 5 days, 8 hours and 38 minutes (av. spd. 21.95 kts). She was the first liner to receive wireless messages from Marconi stations in Nova Scotia and England, providing passengers with a ship's first daily newspaper — the Cunard Daily Bulletin. The *Lucania* was destroyed by fire in Huskisson Dock, Liverpool on 14th August 1909, and sold for scrap to Thomas Ward, Swansea in 1910.

S. S. „Ivernia." Cunard Line.

IVERNIA, 1900-1917

Twin screw steamer. Built in 1900 by C.S. Swan Hunter, Newcastle. 13,799 g.r.t, 9.058 net. 582′ x 64.8′ x 37.6′. Service speed 15kts. Passengers: 164 first class, 200 second class and 1,600 third class. The *Ivernia*'s maiden voyage was from Liverpool-New York on 14th April 1900. Her normal service was Liverpool-Queenstown (Cobh)-Boston. In 1911 New York-Mediterranean service, and 1912 the Fiume-Messina-Palermo-Naples-Funchal-New York service. In 1917 she was torpedoed by UB-47, 58 miles off Cape Matapan, Italy with 2,800 troops on board en-route for Alexandria. 87 troops and 36 crew were lost.

INTERIOR VIEW OF 'IVERNIA' OR 'SAXONIA'

The first-class smoking room of either the *Ivernia* or the *Saxonia* giving a good representation of the high standard of furnishings. The postcard is one of a series of cards by an unknown publisher illustrating the interiors of passenger ships from various companies.

"SAXONIA IN HUSKISSON DOCK, W & CO."

SAXONIA, 1900-1925
Twin screw steamer. Built in 1900 by John Brown & Company, Glasgow. 14,281 g.r.t., 9,100 net.
Same specifications as her sister-ship *Ivernia*.
Her maiden voyage was from Liverpool-Queenstown (Cobh)-Boston on 22nd May 1900. She was used on the winter cruises from New York to the Mediterranean. At the start of the First World War she was used as a troopship and as a German prisoner-of-war ship moored on the River Thames. This postcard by Wright & Co., Bootle shows her being assisted into her berth at Huskisson Dock, Liverpool, assisted by two tugs.

SAXONIA, 1900-1925

The *Saxonia* cost £400,000 to build. Both the *Saxonia* and *Ivernia* had the distinguishing feature of tall funnels; 106 ft high from the main deck to the rim cowl. Before the end of the First World War, in 1917, she sailed on the London-New York and Liverpool-New York route employed as a troopship. After the war she was used on the London-New York route after a major refit which included her funnel being shortened by 16ft. From 1920-25 she was on the Hamburg-New York service and in 1925 she was sold and broken up in Holland. This postcard shows her being edged into Alexandra Dock, Bootle.

Rescuing the 705 survivors of the Titanic, sunk off Halifax, April 15, 1912, 1,600 persons were drowned. Insurance loss, $14,500,000. Published by Joseph Koehler, 150 Park Row, N. Y.

The Carpathia was on her way to the Mediterranean with 200 passengers on board, when Capt. Rostrom received the distress calls from the Titanic, fifty-six miles away.

"S. S. CARPATHIA."

CARPATHIA, 1903-1918

Twin screw steamer. Built in 1902 by C.S. Swan Hunter, Newcastle and completed in 1903. 13,603 g.r.t. 8,600 net. 540' x 64' x 37.3'. Service speed 14 kts. Passengers: 204 first class and 1500 third class (486 in cabins and the remainder in dormitories).

Her maiden voyage was from Liverpool-Queenstown-Boston on 5th May 1903. She served the Liverpool-New York route until 1904, and then commenced services from New York to the Mediterranean ports between 1905 and 1915. She will always be remembered for her dramatic rescue, under the command of Capt. A.H. Rostron, of the 705 survivors from the ill-fated *Titanic* which sank on 15th April 1912. At the end of the First World War, on 17th July 1918, the *Carpathia* was sunk by three torpedoes from the German U-boat, U55, 170 miles west of Bishop Rock. 5 men were lost and 215 were saved by H.M.S. *Snowdrop*.

SKIRMISHER, 1884-1945

Twin screw tender. Built in 1884 by J. & G. Thompson & Co., Glasgow. 612 g.r.t., 194 net. 165′ x 32′ x 15′. Served as Cunard's tender at Liverpool, accommodating 1,200 passengers and their baggage. In 1911, she went to the assistance of the *Mauretania* which had broken her moorings, drifted up river and gone aground on Pluckington Bank. The *Mauretania* was floated off undamaged on the next high tide.

CUNARDER PANNONIA AT FIUME

PANNONIA, 1903-1922

Twin screw steamer. Built in 1903 by John Brown & Co., Glasgow. 9,851 g.r.t., 6,210 net. 486.5′ x 59.2′ x 33′. Service speed 12 kts. Passengers: 91 first class, 71 second class and 2,066 steerage class for emigrants accommodated in dormitories. The *Pannonia* had originally been ordered by Sir Christopher Furness but was purchased on the stocks by Cunard. Fiume-New York service (1904-14), London-New York service (1915-19), Trieste-New York service (1919-21). In 1922 she was sold for breaking up at Hamburg, Germany.

CUNARD R.M.S. "CARMANIA" (TURBINE) AND "CARONIA".

CARONIA and CARMANIA, c.1907

A watercolour postcard, one of a series painted by the artist Odin Rosenvinge. The *Caronia* and the *Carmania* both entered service in 1905. They were used by Cunard as test ships: the *Caronia* fitted with quadruple expansion engines and the *Carmania* fitted with steam turbines. The *Carmania* proving more economical and capable of a slightly higher service speed. Both ships were the first Cunard ships to be fitted with Stone Lloyd watertight doors.

Huskisson Dock and S.S. Caronia, Liverpool.

CARONIA, 1905-1932

Twin screw steamer. Built in 1905 by John Brown & Co., Glasgow. 19,687 g.r.t., 10,306 net. 675' o.a., 650' b.p. x 72.1' x 40.1'. Service speed 18 kts. Passengers: 300 first class, 350 second class and 1,100 third class. Her maiden voyage commenced on 25th February 1905 from Liverpool to New York. She remained on this service, with additional services on the Mediterranean route during winter months, until the outbreak of the First World War. The *Caronia* was converted to an armed merchant cruiser and served as a troopship until 1918. After the war she resumed service and employed on different routes to North America. In 1920 she was converted to oil fuel, and in 1924 the passenger accommodation was remodelled to 425 cabin class, 365 tourist class and 650 third class. *Caronia* was laid up in 1931 and sold in 1932 to Hughes Bolckow for scrapping, resold the same year to Japanese shipbreakers, and renamed *Taiseiyo Maru* for her final journey.

CARMANIA, 1905-1932

Triple screw steamer. Built in 1905 by John Brown & Co., Glasgow. 19,524 g.r.t., 9,982 net. Similar specifications to her sister-ship. Service speed 18½ kts. The first Cunard liner to be fitted with turbines.

The *Carmania's* maiden voyage commenced on 2nd December 1905 from Liverpool to New York. She remained on this service during the summer months, and from New York to the Mediterranean ports during the winter. On 4th June, 1912, she caught fire in Liverpool but was not seriously damaged. At the beginning of the First World War, the *Carmania* was converted to an armed merchant cruiser. On 14th September 1914, off the Brazilian island Trindade, she engaged the *Cap Trafalgar,* the flagship of the German Hamburg-Sud Amerika Line, which had also been converted to an armed merchant cruiser. The two ships suffered heavy gunfire and after one hour and forty minutes the engagement concluded with the *Cap Trafalgar* being sunk. After the war, the *Carmania* resumed service between Liverpool and New York. She made her final voyage in August 1931, then laid up at Sheerness, and during 1932 she was sold to be broken up by the shipbreakers Hughes Bolckow at Blyth.

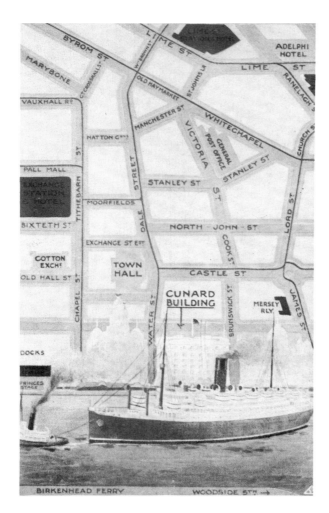

MAP OF LIVERPOOL
An official postcard issued by the Cunard Line showing a map of Liverpool and its main roads, railway stations and tram routes. It also shows the position of the Cunard building situated near the Pier Head, near to the Landing-Stage. A Cunarder is shown in the river being towed by a tug away from the Stage.

Cunard Line Offices Pier Head Liverpool

CUNARD LINE OFFICES, LIVERPOOL

An artist-drawn postcard showing the head offices of the Cunard Line which are situated on the waterfront, near to the Landing-Stage, next to the Royal Liver Buildings. The remarkable building was designed in Italian Rennaissance style, based on the design of the Farnese Palace in Rome, and completed in 1916. The exterior features the coats of arms of this country's allies during the First World War on the frieze on the Pier Head elevation, the coats of arms of the principal sea ports of Great Britain, and nautical emblems and scenes of distant lands provide themes for the doorway and projecting platform. The building is no longer occupied by Cunard and has now been sold.

LUSITANIA, 1907-1915
Quadruple-screw steamer. Built in 1906 by John Brown Ltd., Glasgow. 31,550 g.r.t., 9,145 net. 790′ o.a. 762.1′ b.p. x 87.8′ x 56.5′. Four Parsons steam turbines, with the furnaces burning 850 tons of coal each day. Passengers: 563 first class, 464 second class and 1,138 third class. 800 crew. Service speed 23 kts. When she was launched on 7th June 1906 by Lady Inverclyde, the *Lusitania* was the largest vessel in the world, the first quadruple-screw steamer and the first British four-funnelled steamer. An unusual postcard showing the *Lusitania's* immense size: compare the size of the man on the floor of the graving dock.

LUSITANIA, 1907-1915

The *Lusitania*, the first of two super liners ordered by Cunard, photographed by Wright & Co., Bootle in August 1907. The postcard, postally used on 29th August, shows the liner being manoevured out of the Sandon Basin by four tugs and the Cunard tender *Skirmisher,* prior to her maiden voyage in September from Liverpool to New York via Queenstown.

R.M.S. LUSITANIA.
At Landing Stage
LIVERPOOL.

LUSITANIA, 1907-1915

To accommodate the *Lusitania,* the Mersey Docks & Harbour Board had to remove 200,000 tons of sand from abreast of the Liverpool landing stage. The floating landing-stage was fitted with elevated platforms from which the gangways could reach the upper decks. On her second voyage, in October 1907, the *Lusitania* broke the westbound record for the Blue Riband in a time of 4 days, 19 hours and 52 minutes. (Average speed 23.99 kts), and the same month broke the eastbound record in a time of 4 days 22 hours and 53 minutes (Average speed 23.61 kts). She held the eastbound record until November 1907 and the westbound record until May 1908. She broke the westbound record on two further occasions in July 1908 and 1909, reducing the time to 4 days, 11 hours and 42 minutes (25.85 kts). Notice the laden horse-drawn baggage cart in the foreground.

FIRST CLASS LOUNGE. R.M.S LUSITANIA.

FIRST-CLASS LOUNGE, LUSITANIA

The interior decorations of the *Lusitania* were designed by James Millar, the Scottish architect responsible for the 1901 Glasgow Exhibition. Every effort was made to provide passengers with luxury, grandeur and extravagance. The first-class lounge was designed in Georgian style with the bulkheads and pillars lined with mahogany. The postcard shows part of the skylight containing stained glass depicting the twelve months of the year, and one of the two marble fireplaces with enamel panels by Alexander Fisher. The green carpets and furnishings with a floral design were supplied by Waring and Gillow.

LUSITANIA, 1907-1915

The *Lusitania,* affectionately known as the 'Lucy', edging its way towards the lock gates, assisted by seven tugs and watched by a large crowd on the quayside. On 1st May, 1915, the *Lusitania* sailed from New York on her last voyage with 1,957 passengers and crew on board. On Friday afternoon, 7th May, ten miles off the Old Head of Kinsale in southern Ireland, she was attacked by a torpedo from the German submarine U-20. The torpedo hit the *Lusitania* on the starboard side amidships and following a further explosion from inside the ship — there is some controversy as to whether this was a second torpedo or explosives on board — the *Lusitania* sank within twenty minutes. 1,198 people lost their lives, including 124 Americans. This tragedy aroused great hatred against Germany from the Americans and gradually altered their stand away from neutrality, and eventually to America entering the war against Germany. After the sinking of the *Lusitania,* Cunard suspended all Atlantic passenger services until the end of the war.

"OCEAN MONARCHS"

The *Mauretania* and the *Lusitania* photographed in Canada Dock, Liverpool on 14th October 1909. The two ships also berthed at Sandon Dock. The three tugs in attendance are (left to right): *Alexander*, built in 1906; *Horbey*, built in 1908; and *Trafalgar*, built in 1906. Two gigs complete the picture. The *Mauretania* was named after Roman Morocco and Algeria, and the *Lusitania* was named after Roman Portugal.

Q.T.S.S MAURETANIA. LENGTH 787 X 87 · 6 X 60 · 4'

MAURETANIA, 1907-1935

Quadruple screw steamer. Built by Swan Hunter and Wigham Richardson at Wallsend on Tyne. Launched on 20th September 1906 and completed in October 1907. 31,938 g.r.t., 8,948 net. 787' x 87.6' x 60.4'. Turbines by Wallsend Shipway Co., Newcastle-upon-Tyne. Service speed 24-25 kts. Passengers: 563 first class, 464 second class and 1,138 third class. 812 crew. Photographed at Wallsend during her fitting out before her hull had been painted black.

MAURETANIA, 1907-1935

A rare postcard photographed by Wright & Co., Bootle, posted on 2nd November 1907, and showing the arrival of the *Mauretania* prior to her maiden voyage on 16th November from Liverpool
and Queenstown to New York. On her return from New York in November 1907, she broke the
eastbound record of the Blue Riband in a time of 4 days, 22 hours and 29 mins
(av. spd. 23.69 kts). This eastbound record was then broken a further six times reducing the time
to 4 days, 17 hours, 21 mins. (av. spd. 25.88 kts), and held for 22 years until July 1929. She took
the westbound record in May 1908, losing it to her sister-ship the *Lusitania* in July the same year,
then regaining it in September 1909 with a time of 4 days, 10 hours and 51 mins. (av. spd. 26.06
kts) — a record she held until July 1929, the longest holder of the Blue Riband until the arrival
of the *United States* in 1952.

MAURETANIA, 1907-1935

Mauretania docking in Liverpool, having passed through the Sandon Half-Tide entrance locks, after one of her 269 double crossings of the Atlantic. She is shown being assisted by three tugs: *Herculaneum, Canning* and *Coburg* — all owned by the Alexandra towing company. The *Mauretania* served as a troop transport, and a hospital ship for a short period, during the First World War. She returned to service with Cunard in May 1919 and during a major refit in 1921-22, she was converted from coal to oil fuel. She served as a cruise ship in 1931-34 and on 26th September 1934 she made her last transatlantic voyage. Sold on 2nd April 1935 to Metal Industries Ltd., and scrapped the same year at Rosyth, Scotland. The *Mauretania* became one of the most famous of the Atlantic liners and known as "The Grand Old Lady of the Atlantic" — a legend in her own lifetime.

Cunard R.M.S. Mauretania   SMOKING ROOM   SECOND CLASS

SECOND-CLASS SMOKING ROOM — MAURETANIA

The interior decorations of the *Mauretania* were designed by Harold Peto, who was well known for designing interiors of country houses in Britain and constructed under the supervision of W.C. Phipps, the head foreman joiner at the shipbuilders in Wallsend. The public rooms were designed in either French or Italian styles, with the grand staircase modelled on a fifteen-century Italian example. The dining rooms were panelled in straw-coloured oak and the state-rooms were designed in the style of Adams, Sheraton or Chippendale. The best English and French woods were used for the wood veneers and carvings were cut back from the face of solid wood. All the lavatory fittings were white metal; the first-class state-rooms and royal suite silver-plated. Both the *Lusitania* and *Mauretania* were very similarly designed providing passengers with superb luxury.

39

ROYAL VISIT TO R.M.S. MAURETANIA, 1913
The first phase of Gladstone Dock, Bootle was opened by Their Majesties George V and Queen Mary in July 1913. During their visit they viewed the *Mauretania*. This photographic postcard by Wright & Co., Bootle shows the King inspecting the ships' stokers on deck.

ROYAL VISIT TO R.M.S. MAURETANIA, 1927

The second phase of the construction of Gladstone Dock, Bootle was opened by King George V and Queen Mary in 1927. The opening ceremony comprised of a ribbon, stretched across the mouth of the dock, which was broken by the Mersey Docks and Harbour Board's tender *Galatea,* conveying the royal party and dignitaries, as it passed the dock entrance. This postcard shows the King and Queen boarding the *Mauretania* from the *Galatea* after the ceremony.

LIVERPOOL *from the Air.*

LIVERPOOL FROM THE AIR

At the beginning of this century, Liverpool had become the nation's second port (after London) and possessed one of the most impressive waterfronts in Britain: six-and-a-half miles of docks from Gladstone Dock to Dingle Oil Jetty alone, not including the Garston Docks, Birkenhead Docks or the docks on the southern side of the Mersey estuary stretching towards the entrance of the Manchester Ship Canal. The panorama shows from top left to bottom right: Trafalgar Dock, Victoria Dock, Princes Dock, the Landing-Stage (the largest floating structure in the world) and Riverside Station, the Royal Liver Buildings, the Cunard Building, the Dock offices of the Mersey Docks and Harbour Board, Canning Dock, Half Tide Dock, and in the foreground the Albert Dock.

RIVERSIDE STATION, LIVERPOOL.

RIVERSIDE STATION, c.1910

After docking at the landing stage, transatlantic passengers, who were travelling on to London, would disembark and pass through the Custom and Transit sheds, and then cross Princes Parade to Riverside Station where a train would be waiting to convey them on the final stages of their journey. This postcard shows Princes Parade with a liner at the stage, and carriages lined up awaiting passengers to transport them to Liverpool's city centre hotels. The entrance to Riverside Station is on the right.

Riverside Railway Station. LIVERPOOL.

RIVERSIDE STATION, c.1908

An interior view of Riverside Station. Two L. & N.W.R. saddle-tank engines head a line of carriages brought to the station prior to their departure to London by an express steam locomotive. After leaving Riverside Station, the train crossed the swing-bridge at Princes Dock and wound its way slowly through the dock estate, across Waterloo Road, through Waterloo Tunnel, eventually emerging at Edge Hill Station and then continuing on to London. Riverside Station closed in 1971.

CUNARD LINER R.M.S. "FRANCONIA"

FRANCONIA, 1911-1916

Twin screw steamer. Built by Swan Hunter & Wigham Richardson at Wallsend and completed in January 1911.
18,150 g.r.t. 625' x 71'. Service speed 16 kts. Passengers: 300 first class, 350 second class and 2,200 third class.
Her maiden voyage commenced on 25th February 1911 from Liverpool to New York. She was requisitioned by
the Government as a troop transport on 15th February 1915 and sunk by U47 on 4th October 1916, 200 miles
north-east of Malta. Twelve people lost their lives.

This type of card came into prominence with the vast number of emigrations to America and the Commonwealth.
Many different colourful designs exist showing clasped hands, national symbols and the means of transport. This
postcard showing the *Franconia* would have been on sale on board the ship and posted to friends and relatives
by the passengers who were starting a new life, attracted by the promises of wealth and new opportunities.

ROYAL GEORGE, 1916-1922

Triple screw steamer. Built in 1907 by the Fairfield Company, Glasgow. 11,146 g.r.t., 5,685 net. Three steam turbines. Service speed 18 kts. 525.7′ x 60.1′ x 27′. Built originally for the Egyptian Mail S.S. Co for the Marseilles — Alexandria service and named the *Heliopolis*. 1910 — Sold to Canadian Northern Steamships, Toronto who renamed her the *Royal George*. In 1916, Cunard bought Canadian Northern Steamships and thereby took over the *Royal George*. Sold in 1922 and broken up at Wilhelmshaven, Germany.

EMPRESS OF AUSTRALIA
21,000 TONS

MAJESTIC 56,000 TONS

HOMERIC
34,000 TONS

AQUITANIA
45,000 TONS

BERENGARIA
52,000 TONS

EMPRESS OF BRITAIN
42,000 TONS

MAURETANIA
30,000 TONS

ARANDORA STAR
14,000 TONS

ALCANTARA
22,000 TONS

1203 C. R. Hoffmann AERIAL VIEW OF SOUTHAMPTON DOCKS, SHOWING NINE OF THE WORLD'S LARGEST LINERS
Southampton   GROSS TONNAGE 316,000 TONS.

SOUTHAMPTON DOCKS

Southampton advertised itself as the "Gateway to the World". Southampton's Ocean Dock, which
was opened in 1911, was the main dock for the White Star Line and later the Cunard Line. Some
of the services were switched from Liverpool, much to the consternation of Liverpudlians, to
Southampton mainly because of its geographical location. This postcard by C.R. Hoffman of
Southampton shows an aerial view of the docks with some of the largest liners in the world,
including, *Aquitania, Mauretania, and Berengaria.*

47

CUNARD POSTER, c. 1920s

This striking and dramatic publicity poster, issued by the Cunard Line, shows the three major ships of the company, at the time: *Mauretania, Berengaria* and *Aquitania*. The poster reproduced as a postcard was sold on board the ships and from agents and company offices.

1028 C. R. Hoffmann,
Southampton.

R.M.S. "BERENGARIA." 52,226 Tons.
Length 919 Ft. Breadth 98 Ft

BERENGARIA, 1921-1938

Quadruple screw steamer. Launched at Vulkan Werke, Hamburg on 23 May 1912 as the *Imperator;* one of three superliners for Albert Ballin's Hamburg-American Line — the others being *Bismark* and *Vaterland.* When completed in April 1913 she was the largest ship in the world, but superseded by her sister-ships when they were completed: the *Bismark* (56,000 tons) remained the world's largest ship for nineteen years. The *Imperator*'s specifications were 52,226 g.r.t., 21,506 net. 919.2' o.a., 882' b.p. x 98.3' x 57.1'. Service speed 22 kts., Passengers: 979 first class, 830 second class and 1,000 third class. 950 crew. During the First World War, she was laid up in the Elbe river until 1919. She was ceded to Great Britain after the Treaty of Versailles, chartered by Cunard from the Shipping Controller, and later purchased by Cunard in February 1921.

49

BERENGARIA, 1921-1938

The *Imperator's* first voyage for Cunard commenced on 21st February 1920 from Liverpool to New York, and on 16th April 1921 she was renamed the *Berengaria* — the wife of Richard the Lion Heart. One of the biggest problems Cunard had with the ship was to correct her permanent list and to stop her rolling badly in heavy seas. Marble bath tubs were replaced with metal tubs in the first-class cabins and ballast of pig iron was added to her concrete ballast. In May 1922 she was converted to oil fuel. In 1929, she became the first ship to have a stock exchange on board, but this was soon terminated following the Wall Street Crash. During the 1930s, she provided $50 "booze cruises" from New York, following the depression and during the prohibition era. The *Berengaria* remained Cunard's flagship until the building of the *Queen Mary.*

The postcard shows the first-class lounge, lavishly decorated using the finest materials and craftsmen. Notice the stained-glass skylight.

BERENGARIA, 1921-1938

An interior view showing the Palm Court which possessed another fine ceiling, semi-carpeted floor and the finest cane furniture.

On 3rd March, 1938, the passenger accommodation was badly damaged by fire in New York and the *Berengaria* returned to Southampton on her last voyage without passengers. Sold on 7th November 1938 to ship-breakers, J. Jarvis of Jarrow, and finally dismantled after the Second World War in 1946.

CUNARD LINER "AQUITANIA" LEAVING WAYS—ENTERING WATER

AQUITANIA, 1914-1950

Quadruple screw steamer. Built by John Brown & Co., Clydebank, launched in April 1913 by the Countess of Derby and completed in May 1914. 45,647 g.r.t., 21,998 net. 901′ o.a., 868.6′ b.p. x 97′ x 49.7′. Service speed 23 kts. Passengers: 618 first class, 614 second class and 1,998 third class. Crew 972. The last Cunarder with four funnels.

AQUITANIA, 1914-1950

The *Aquitania's* maiden voyage commenced on 30th May 1914 from Liverpool to New York via Queenstown. After completing three round trips to New York, she was requistitioned by the Government at the beginning of the First World War and converted to an armed merchant cruiser. After a collision with the Leyland liner *Canadian* in August 1914, she was laid up until early 1915 then used as a troop ship during the Dardanelles campaign. The *Aquitania* was then used as a hospital ship in the Mediterranean until 1917, and for the rest of the war she was used as a troop ship. She commenced regular services again with Cunard on 14th June 1919.

AQUITANIA, 1914-1950
A publicity postcard published by Cunard showing a cut-away view of the interior of the *Aquitania*. From top to bottom, the postcard shows: the first-class accommodation, second-class accommodation, third-class accommodation, the storage areas, and the engine room.

AQUITANIA, 1914-1950

The *Aquitania* was one of the most beautiful ships built by Cunard. It was designed in a variety of period and classical styles; the postcard showing the ornate Carolean smoking room. In 1920, the *Aquitania* was converted from coal to oil and also became the first merchant ship to be fitted with a gyro compass. In 1936, she provided valuable test data for the Queen Mary, when she was fitted with new style propellors; resulting in 2½ knots extra speed without consuming extra fuel.

AQUITANIA, 1914-1950

At the beginning of the Second World War, the *Aquitania* was requisitioned by the Government as a troop ship and continued in this capacity until 1948. She returned to Cunard and after twelve voyages to Halifax under contract with the Canadian government, she made her last voyage to Southampton which ended on 1st December 1949. Sold in February 1950 to the British Iron and Steel Corporation and finally broken up at Gareloch, Scotland.

During her long service, the *Aquitania,* known as 'The Ship Beautiful', steamed 3 million miles, carried 1,200,000 passengers, crossed the Atlantic 475 times, and served in two world wars.

THE NEW CUNARDER "ALBANIA." CANADIAN SERVICE

ALBANIA, 1921-1941

Twin screw steamer. Built in 1921 by Scotts SB & E Company, Greenock. Tonnage: 12,767 g.r.t., 7,519 net. 523.1′ x 64′ x 43.9′. Oil-fired steam turbines. 500 cabin-class passengers and cargo. The first of Cunard's replacement programme after the First World War. Sold in 1930 and renamed *California* by Navigazione Libera Triestina. On 11th August, 1941, she was torpedoed and sunk by British aircraft at Syracuse, Sicily. Refloated but later scrapped.

SCYTHIA, 1921-1958

Twin screw steamer. Built by Vickers Armstrong, Barrow-in-Furness, but completed in Lorient in December 1920. Tonnage: 19,730 g.r.t., 11,927 net. 625′ o.a., 600.7′ b.p x 73.8′ x 40.8′. Steam turbines. Service speed 16 kts. Passengers: 350 first class, 350 second class, 1,500 third class. 434 crew. Her maiden voyage commenced on 20th August 1921 from Liverpool to New York. She remained on this service for many years, calling at Boston on the outward and return journeys. Damaged in October 1923 when in a collision with the White Star liner *Cedric*. Served as a troop ship during the Second World War and seriously damaged by bombing in November 1942. Repaired and continued in Goverment service until October 1949. After a full refit she returned to Cunard service until October 1957. Collided with Canadian collier *Wabana* on 5th June 1952; both ships blamed for incorrect use of radar. Chartered by Canadian government from October to December 1957, then departed to Inverkeithing, Scotland on 1st January 1958 for scrapping.

SAMARIA, 1921-1956

Twin screw steamer. Sister-ship to *Scythia* and *Laconia*. Built by Cammell Laird, Birkenhead and completed August 1921. Tonnage: 19,597 g.r.t., 11,834 net. 626′ o.a., 601.5′ b.p. x 74′. Steam turbines. Service speed 16 kts. Passengers: 350 first class, 350 second class, 1,500 third class, 434 crew. Engaged on a similar service as *Scythia*. During the Second World War, she served as a troop ship and remained in Government use until September 1948. Returned to Cunard service and served on the London to Montreal route. Major refit in 1950. Routed from Southampton in July 1951. Represented Cunard at the Coronation Review, Spithead in 1953. Her last voyage for Cunard commenced in November 1955 and she was sold in January 1956 for scrapping at Inverkeithing, Scotland.

ABSTRACT OF LOG OF THE
CUNARD WHITE STAR R.M.S. "SAMARIA."

Captain—J. McROSTIE

NEW YORK (via Boston, Greenock & Dublin) TO LIVERPOOL

1938	RUNS	LAT. N.	LONG. W.	WEATHER, ETC.
June 17	—	—	—	At 5.00 p.m. D.S.T. left Company's Pier New York
,, 17	—	—	—	At 6.54 p.m. D.S.T **Ambrose Channel L.V. abeam (Departure)**
,, 18	345	New York	to Boston	At 3.23 p.m. D.S T. Boston L.V. abeam, Arrival
,, 18				At 11.29 p.m. D.S.T. **Boston L.V. abeam (Departure)**
,, 19	210	42.52	66.03	Light breeze, smooth sea, cloudy with misty patches
,, 20	389	44.05	57.18	Light breeze, slight sea and swell, overcast, misty patches
,, 21	401	46.12	48.27	Light airs, smooth sea, overcast, fine and clear
,, 22	391	49.32	40.06	Moderate breeze mod sea, slight swell, cloudy, fine & clear
,, 23	393	52.28	30.48	Moderate breeze, mod. sea slight swell, mainly, o'cast, clear
,, 24	400	54.26	20.06	Strong following breeze, rough sea and swell, cloudy, clear
,, 25	393	55.22	8.50	Strong following breeze, rough sea and swell, cloudy, clear
,, 26	168	To Greenock	—	At 9.39 p.m. B.S..T. **Cloch Point, Greenock (Arrival)**
	2745			

Length of Passage—Boston Light Vessel to Cloch Point : —6 days, 17 hours, 10 mins.
Average Speed 17.04 knots.

ABSTRACT FROM THE LOG OF R.M.S. SAMARIA

Cunard R.M.S. Samaria

FIRST-CLASS DINING ROOM

INTERIOR OF FIRST-CLASS DINING ROOM, R.M.S. SAMARIA

61

LACONIA, 1922-1942

Twin screw steamer. Sister ship to the *Scythia* and *Samaria*. Built by Swan Hunter and Wigham Richardson, Tyneside, and completed in January 1922. Tonnage: 19,695 g.r.t., 11,804 net. 623' o.a. 601.3 b.p. x 73'. Steam turbines. Service speed 16 kts. Passengers: 347 first class, 350 second class and 1,500 third class, 434 crew. Her maiden voyage commenced on 25th May 1922 from Southampton to New York, and then served on the New York service from Liverpool and also Hamburg in 1923. During the 1930s, she served as a cruise ship. Requisitioned during the Second World War by the Government. On 12th September 1942, off Freetown, West Africa, she was torpedoed by U-156. When the U-boat commander discovered she was carrying 1,800 Italian prisoners of war, and after receiving permission from the German Naval Command, he assisted in the rescue of the men along with U-506 and U-507. Four days later, when a Liberator plane attacked U-156, the German commander abandoned the survivors. After this incident, U-boats were ordered not to assist survivors in the future.

FREIGHT PUBLICITY POSTER
For Cunard-White Star Line,
March 1950

Cunard Freight Services
CUNARD WHITE STAR
LIVERPOOL SAILINGS

M.V. "BRITANNIC" 27,000 Tons

LIVERPOOL TO NEW YORK

		Receiving Cargo
*BRITANNIC (via COBH)		MAR. 17th to MAR. 25th (noon)
MEDIA		MAR. 27th to MAR. 30th (noon)
PARTHIA		APR. 3rd to APR. 13th (noon)

LIVERPOOL TO BOSTON

MEDIA (via NEW YORK)	MAR. 20th to MAR. 29th (noon)
PARTHIA (via NEW YORK)	APR. 3rd to APR. 12th (noon)

LIVERPOOL TO HALIFAX, N.S.

ARABIA	MAR. 10th to MAR. 22nd (noon)

LIVERPOOL TO SAINT JOHN, N.B.

ARABIA (via HALIFAX, N.S.)	MAR. 10th to MAR. 22nd (noon)

LIVERPOOL TO MONTREAL

VASCONIA	MAR. 23rd to APR. 1st (noon)

LIVERPOOL TO QUEBEC

FRANCONIA	APR. 1st to APR. 5th (noon)

Loading Berths: Huskisson Dock and * Gladstone Dock.

Goods for BERMUDA, REPUBLIC OF COLOMBIA, WEST INDIES, CENTRAL AMERICA, WEST COAST OF SOUTH AMERICA
with transhipment at New York carried on through bills of lading obtainable from Agents of the on-carrying lines.
All bookings are conditional upon the vessel named being available for the voyage, and goods are received for shipment
only subject to the terms and conditions of the Company's usual Form of Wharfinger's Receipt and/or Bill of Lading. They are
also subject to any direction or control by the Government of any nation and to North Atlantic Westbound Freight Association
War clauses.

THE CUNARD STEAM-SHIP COMPANY LIMITED,

R.M.S. "Antonia"

ANTONIA, 1922-1942
Built by Vickers Armstrong Ltd., Barrow-in-Furness. Tonnage: 13,867 g.r.t., 8,445 net. Similar specifications to *Andania*. Her maiden voyage commenced on 15th June 1922 serving similar routes as her sister ship *Andania*. Requisitioned by the Government and altered to an armed merchant cruiser in 1940. Sold to the Admiralty in March 1942 and converted to a repair ship. Renamed H.M.S. *Wayland* in 1944. Scrapped in 1948.

CUNARD LINE R.M.S. "ANTONIA."

(Captain G. W. MELSOM, O.B.E., R.N.R.)

ABSTRACT OF LOG.

MONTREAL & QUEBEC TO GREENOCK, BELFAST AND LIVERPOOL

Date 1930			Dist.	Latitude N.	Longitude W.	Weather, etc.
Fri.	August	29				At 11-34 a.m. C.S.T., departure Montreal
,,	,,	29	136	To Quebec		At 10-00 p.m. C.S.T., arrived Quebec
,,	,,	29				At 10-40 p.m. C.S.T., left Quebec
Sat.	,,	30	154	To Father Point		At 8-16 a.m. C.S.T., (12-16 p.m. G.M.T.), Father Point abeam—departure
,,	,,	30	60	49.02½	67.12	Moderate sea, fine, clear and cloudy
Sun.	,,	31	357	50.34	58.39	Light breeze, slight sea, occasional misty patches
Mon.	Sept.	1	291	52.40	51.42	Smooth sea, overcast and clear, long periods dense fog
Tues.	,,	2	350	54.39	42.25	Light breeze, slight sea and swell, cloudy and clear
Wed.	,,	3	350	55.56	32.25	Moderate breeze, sea and swell, overcast, rain
Thurs.	,,	4	353	56.17	21.54	Moderate breeze and sea, overcast, rain and drizzle
Fri.	,,	5	363	55.47	11.07	Fresh breeze, moderate sea, overcast, misty, rain
Sat.	,,	6	248	To Kempock Point		At 5-11 a.m., G.M.T., Kempock Point abeam (arrival)
			2372			

Length of Passage—Father Point to Kempock Point—**6 days, 16 hours, 55 minute.**
Average Speed—**14.77 knots.**   **Detention 22 minutes.**

ABSTRACT FROM LOG, R.M.S. ANTONIA
(29th August — 6th September 1930)

**PASSENGER LIST BOOKLET,
R.M.S. ANTONIA**
The front cover illustrating the
emblem of the Cunard Line

List of Passengers

R.M.S.
"ANTONIA"

Twin Screw — Gross Tonnage, 13,867

———

CAPTAIN—G. W. MELSOM, R.N.R.

OFFICERS

Ch. Engineer	W. Booth	Ch Officer	W. H. Poole, R.D., R.N.R.
Surgeon	P. B. P. Mellows	Purser	C. E. F. Chubb
Ch. Steward	H. Tweed	Asst. Purser	C. F. Doughty

Tourist Third Cabin Purser   R. P. Cahan

Tourist Third Cabin Steward   T. Watterson

Conductress   Miss E. Browne

———

SAILING FROM

MONTREAL TO LIVERPOOL
VIA
GLASGOW AND BELFAST

———

FRIDAY, AUGUST 29TH, 1930

SUMMARY OF 1930-31 CRUISES FROM NEW YORK

STEAMER	DATE	AUSPICES
AROUND THE WORLD		
"SAMARIA"	December 3rd	Cunard Line & Thos. Cook & Son
"FRANCONIA"	January 10th	Cunard Line & Thos. Cook & Son
AFRICAN		
"TRANSYLVANIA"	January 17th	Cunard-Anchor Lines & American Express Co
MEDITERRANEAN		
"SCYTHIA"	January 27th	Frank Tourist Company
"CARINTHIA"	January 31st	Raymond & Whitcomb Co.
"MAURETANIA"	February 21st	Cunard Line
"CARINTHIA"	April 14th	Raymond & Whitcomb Co.
NORTH CAPE		
"FRANCONIA"	June 24th	Raymond & Whitcomb Co.
"CARINTHIA"	June 30th	Raymond & Whitcomb Co.
WEST INDIES		
"FRANCONIA"	November 18th	Cunard Line
"FRANCONIA"	December 2nd	Cunard Line
"CARINTHIA"	December 18th	Bramson Co.
"FRANCONIA"	December 20th	Cunard Line
"CAMERONIA"	December 24th	National Tours
"CARINTHIA"	January 10th	Cunard Line
"CALEDONIA"	January 24th	Anchor Line
"CALEDONIA"	February 14th	Anchor Line
"AURANIA"	March 14th	Cunard Line
"AURANIA"	March 31st	Cunard Line
"CALIFORNIA"	April 3rd	National Tours
"CALEDONIA"	April 3rd	National Tours

HAVANA

"CARONIA"		"CARMANIA"	
From New York	From Havana	From New York	From Havana
December 27th	January 1st	January 17th	January 20th
January 10th	January 15th	January 24th	January 27th
January 21st	January 24th	January 31st	February 3rd
January 28th	January 31st	February 7th	February 10th
February 4th	February 7th	February 18th	February 21st
February 14th	February 17th	February 25th	February 28th
February 21st	February 24th	March 4th	March 7th
February 28th	March 3rd	March 11th	March 17th
March 7th	March 10th		

"MAURETANIA"			
From New York	February 11th	From Havana	February 15th

EXTRACTS FROM PASSENGER BOOKLET, R.M.S ANTONIA

R. M. S. LANCASTRIA.

LANCASTRIA, 1922-1940

Twin screw steamer. Built in 1922 by William Beardmore & Co., Glasgow. Originally planned for the Anchor Line but purchased by Cunard before completion. Tonnage: 16,243 g.r.t., 9,645 net. 578′ o.a., 552.7′ b.p. x 70.4′ x 38.8′. Service speed 16 knots. Passengers: 265 first class, 370 second class, 1,150 third class. 320 crew. Named *Tyrrhenia* (nick-named 'Soup Turren') and renamed *Lancastria* in 1924. Her maiden voyage commenced on 13th June 1922 from Glasgow to Quebec and Montreal. 1923 transferred to Hamburg, Southampton and New York service. 1926 transferred to London, Le Havre, Southampton and New York service. During the 1930s, her hull was painted white and she provided cruises to the Mediterranean, the West Indies and South America.

LANCASTRIA, 1922-1940

The *Lancastria* aground off Egremont in the River Mersey on 20th October 1936. At the beginning of the Second World War she was requisitioned as a troop ship. On 17th June 1940, at anchor off St Nazaire and packed with over 9,000 troops and civilians, the *Lancastria* was attacked by German bombers. Following four direct hits, she sank within twenty minutes. Only 4,000 survived; one of the largest losses of life at sea during the Second World War.

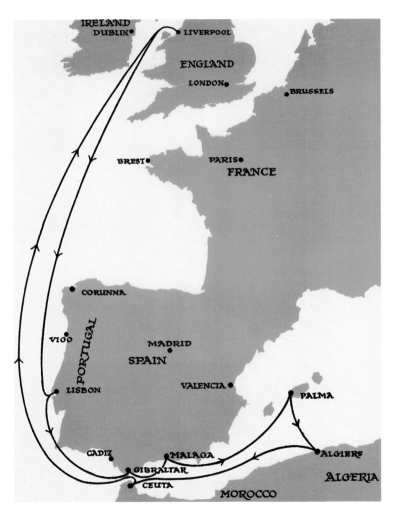

EXTRACT FROM CRUISE BROCHURE, LANCASTRIA,
1932

A 14-day cruise from Liverpool to the Mediterranean, during the first two weeks of September 1932 would have cost from 15 guineas (£15.75) per person for the cheapest rate on D Deck rising to 55 guineas (£57.75) per person for the best cabin on A Deck.

Those were the days!

FRANCONIA, 1923-1956

Twin screw steamer. Built in 1923 by John Brown & Co., Clydebank. Tonnage: 20,175 g.r.t., 12,162 net. 625′ o.a., 601.2′ b.p. x 73.7′ x 40.5′. Service speed 16 kts. Passengers: 350 first class, 350 second class and 1,500 third class, 450 crew. Her maiden voyage commenced in June 1923 from Liverpool to New York, and during the winter months she provided winter cruises.

S.S. FRANCONIA.
ON WORLD CRUISE.
PASSING THE HARBOR BRIDGE. SYDNEY. N.S.W. 2.3.34.

FRANCONIA, 1923-1956

In 1931, the *Franconia* was chartered to the Furness-Bermuda Line for five months and cruised from New York to Bermuda. During the 1930s she served a variety of transatlantic routes and many cruises. This postcard shows the *Franconia* assisted by a tug having passed Sydney Harbour Bridge, during one of her world cruises, on 2nd March 1934.

FRANCONIA, 1923-1956

A round-the-world cruise on the *Franconia* in 1939 was advertised from 410 guineas per person. Passengers departed from Southampton on 24th December 1938 and arrived back in Liverpool on 12th June 1939, having visited 38 ports of call and travelled 44,330 nautical miles. Requisitioned by the Government during the Second World War. In 1945, she served as the British H.Q. during the Yalta conference between Churchill, Roosevelt and Stalin. After the war, in 1949, she returned to the Liverpool, Quebec and Montreal service. Sold in 1956 for breaking up at T.W. Ward's yard at Inverkeithing.

CARINTHIA, 1925-1940

Twin screw steamer. Sister ship to *Franconia*. Originally named *Servia* but renamed *Carinthia* before launching. Built and completed in August 1925 by Vickers Armstrong, Barrow-in-Furness. Tonnage: 20,277 g.r.t., 12,086 net. 624' o.a., 600.6' b.p. x 73.7' x 40.5'. Service speed 16 knots. Passengers: 240 first class, 460 second class and 950 third class. 450 crew. Her maiden voyage commenced on 22nd August 1925 from Liverpool to New York. Employed on this route with *Franconia,* with cruising during the winter months. Between 1925 and 1933, she made a world cruise each year. 1933-36: transatlantic service. 1936-39: cruising from New York to the West Indies. Requisitioned at the beginning of the Second World War by the Government. Torpedoed by U-46 off the west coast of Ireland on 6th June 1940; sinking thirty hours later.

ALAUNIA, 1925-1944

Twin screw steamer. Sister ship to *Ascania* and *Aurania*. Built in 1925 by John Brown & Co., Clydebank. Tonnage: 14,013 g.r.t., 8,437 net. 538' o.a., 520' b.p. x 65.1' x 39.1'. Passengers: 500 cabin class, 1,200 third class, 270 crew. Her maiden voyage commenced on 24th July 1925 from Liverpool to Quebec and Montreal.

Converted to an armed merchant cruiser in 1939. Sold to the Admiralty in 1944, converted to a heavy repair ship, renamed H.M.S. *Alaunia* and stationed at Devonport. Broken up at Blyth in 1957.

R.M.S. "AURANIA".

AURANIA, 1924-1942

Twin screw steamer. Built in 1924 by Swan Hunter & Wigham Richardson. Similar specifications to *Ascania* and *Alaunia*. Her maiden voyage commenced on 13th September 1924 from Liverpool to New York. Converted to an armed merchant cruiser in 1939. During escort duty with a convoy she collided with an iceberg, but only sustained minor damage. Sold to the Admiralty in March 1942, converted to a heavy repair ship and renamed H.M.S. *Artifex*. In 1961, she was sold for breaking up at La Spezia. This postcard shows *Aurania* at the Landing Stage, Liverpool with the Cunard tender *Skirmisher* in attendance (c. 1930)

ASCANIA, 1925-1956

Twin screw steamer. Built and completed in 1925 by W. Armstrong Whitworth & Co., Newcastle. Similar specifications to *Alaunia* and *Aurania*. Her maiden voyage commenced on 22nd May 1925 from London and Southampton to Quebec and Montreal. During the Second World War she was employed as an armed merchant cruiser safely escorting over one thousand ships in various convoys. Converted to an infantry landing ship and assisted in the landings at Sicily, Anzio and southern France. Returned to Cunard in 1947 with a major refit in 1949-50. Her last voyage for Cunard commenced on 26th October 1956 and then requisitioned by the Government as a troopship during the Suez crisis. Sold in 1956 for scrapping at Cashmores in Newport, South Wales.

BRITANNIC, 1930-1960

Twin screw motor-ship. Built and completed in 1930 by Harland Wolff, Belfast for the White Star Line. Tonnage: 26,943 g.r.t., 16,445 net. 683.9′ x 82.5′ x 52.9′. Service speed 18 knots. Diesel engines; 20,000 b.h.p. At the time, Britain's largest motor-ship. Her forward 27ft-high funnel was a dummy; housing water tanks and the engineers' smoking room. Her maiden voyage commenced in 1930 from Liverpool, Glasgow, Belfast to New York. Remained in profitable service across the Atlantic, alternating with cruising in the winter months, until Cunard merged with White Star in 1934. Requisitioned as a troop ship in 1939. She survived the war unscathed, and after a major refit, she returned to Cunard in May 1948. She continued both on Atlantic service and cruising for the next twelve years. Following severe damage to her crankshaft, Cunard sold her in November 1960 to Ward's Shipbreakers, Inverkeithing; the last of the the White Star Liners.

ANDANIA, 1922-1940

Twin screw steamer. Sister ship to *Antonia* and *Ausonia*. Built in 1922 by Hawthorne, Leslie & Co., Newcastle. Tonnage: 13,950 g.r.t., 8,391 net. 538′ o.a., 520.1′ b.p. x 65.3 x 39.1. Service speed 15 knots. Passengers: 486 first class and 1,187 third class. 270 crew. Her maiden voyage commenced on 1st June 1922 from London and Southampton to Quebec and Montreal. 1925-26 transferred to the Hamburg, Southampton and New York service. 1927 transferred to Liverpool to Montreal and Quebec (summer) and Liverpool to Halifax, Nova Scotia (winter). Armed as a merchant cruiser in 1939 and torpedoed on 15th June 1940 by U-70 off Iceland, sinking the following day.

GEORGIC, 1932-1956

Twin screw motor ship. Sister-ship to *Britannic* and the last ship to be built for the White Star Line. Built by Harland and Wolff, Belfast. Tonnage: 27,759 g.r.t., 16,839 net. 682.8′ o.a. x 82.5′ x 52.9′. Diesel engines. Service Speed 18 knots. Slightly different to *Britannic* with increased passenger accommodation and curved bridge front. Passengers: 479 cabin class, 557 tourist class and 506 third class. 505 crew. She entered service in 1932 from Liverpool to New York and became part of the Cunard-White Star fleet when the two companies merged in 1934. Converted to a troopship in March 1940 and assisted in the evacuation of British troops during the Norwegian campaign of the same year. Seriously damaged by bombing in the Suez Canal in July 1941. Towed to India for repairs. Returned to H. & W., Belfast and rebuilt as a troopship, with only one mast and no dummy funnel. After the war, she returned to service after a refit by Palmer & Co., Hebburn-on-Tyne in 1948. In addition to transatlantic voyages, she made many voyages carrying emigrants to Australia and New Zealand. Sold in January 1956 to Shipbreaking Industries of Faslane, Scotland for scrapping.

QUEEN MARY, 1936-1967

Laid down in December 1930 as number 534 at John Brown & Co., Clydebank, Glasgow. A year later, due to the economic depression, work on the ship was cancelled for two-and-a-half years. Following the Government's offer of financial help, and after insisting that the company merge with White Star, work restarted in April 1934. Number 534 was named *Queen Mary* and the great liner was launched by H.M. Queen Mary on 26th September 1934: the first time the Queen of Great Britain had launched a merchant ship. Twenty months later she was completed and the *Queen Mary* set sail on her maiden voyage from Southampton via Cherbourg to New York on 27th May 1936.

QUEEN MARY, 1936-1967
Quadruple screw steamer. Tonnage:
81,237 g.r.t., 34,120 net. 1,020' x 118'
x 68.5'. 14 decks, 16 turbines providing 200,000 s.h.p. Service speed
29 knots. Passengers: 776 cabin class,
784 tourist class, 579 third class,
1,285 crew. During the construction
of the *Queen Mary* , 10 million rivets
and 70,000 gallons of paint were
used, and 4,000 miles of electric cable
were laid.

1270 C. R. Hoffmann, Southampton.

CUNARD WHITE STAR LINER "QUEEN MARY."
The World's Largest and Fastest Liner.
CABIN RESTAURANT.

80,773 Tons

QUEEN MARY, 1936-1967

The interior decoration of the *Queen Mary* was undertaken by 40 contemporary artists and designers; the end result producing a variety of individual styles. Among the record-breaking requirements for the super-liner were: 6 miles of carpets and rugs; 8,500 bed coverlets; 5,600 blankets; 92,000 serviettes; 210,000 towels; 31,000 pillow cases; 10 miles of fabrics; 30,000 sheets; 16,000 pieces of cutlery; and 100,000 pieces of china and glass. The supplies for a single voyage included: 4,000 gallons of milk; 70,000 eggs; 2,000 lb of cheese; 6,000 gallons of beer; 20 tons of fish; 10,000 lbs of sugar; 20,000 packets of cigarettes; and 30 tons of potatoes.

CABIN LOUNGE. R.M.S."QUEEN MARY."

QUEEN MARY, 1936-1967

One of the early problems the *Queen Mary* encountered was a tendency to roll heavily in bad weather. Shortly after her maiden voyage, she was withdrawn from service and the problem was pinpointed to the ship being bottom heavy; the 24 boilers and engines were too low in the ship. After an extensive refit and additional ballast, the problem was finally corrected. In August 1936 she took the westbound record for the Blue Riband from the *Normandie* in a time of 4 days and 27 minutes (av. spd. 30.14 kts). The *Normandie* recaptured the record in July 1937, but in August 1938, the record was regained by the *Queen Mary* in a time of 3 days, 21 hours and 48 minutes (30.99 kts). She also held the eastbound record in August 1936 (30.63 kts), losing it also to the *Normandie* in March 1937, but regaining in August 1938 with a time of 3 days, 20 hours and 42 minutes (31.69 kts). These records were only eclipsed by the *United States* in July 1952.

BRITAINS LARGEST MILLERS
DELIVER FLOUR TO BRITAINS LARGEST SHIP

QUEEN MARY, 1936-1967

Converted to a troop ship in Australia in 1940. Her only wartime accident occurred when she collided with and sliced through her escort H.M.S. *Curacoa* on 2nd October, 1942, off the north-west coast of Ireland. The escort sank within minutes with the loss of 338 lives. She survived the war because of her superior speed and safely transported thousands of troops across the Atlantic. After the war, she returned to John Brown's yard for conversion back to a passenger liner and commenced transatlantic services on 31st July 1947. By the 1960s, fewer people were travelling across the Atlantic by sea, and the *Queen Mary* was eventually sold by Cunard in 1967 for $3.5 million to the city of Long Beach. After completing 1,000 Atlantic crossings she departed from Southampton on 31st October, 1967 for Long Beach, California. After four years as a maritime museum, she was resold and converted to a floating hotel and conference centre.

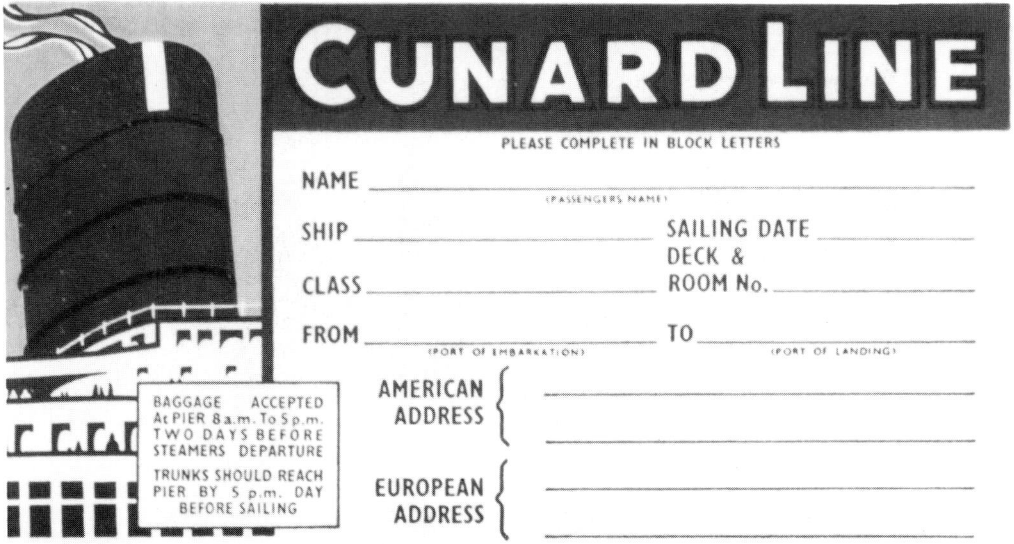

PLEASE COMPLETE IN BLOCK LETTERS

NAME _____
(PASSENGERS NAME)

SHIP _____ SAILING DATE _____

DECK &

CLASS _____ ROOM No. _____

FROM _____ TO _____
(PORT OF EMBARKATION)   (PORT OF LANDING)

AMERICAN { _____
ADDRESS { _____

EUROPEAN { _____
ADDRESS { _____

BAGGAGE ACCEPTED
At PIER 8 a.m. To 5 p.m.
TWO DAYS BEFORE
STEAMERS DEPARTURE
TRUNKS SHOULD REACH
PIER BY 5 p.m. DAY
BEFORE SAILING

CUNARD LINE

FRONT OF CUNARD LUGGAGE LABEL

MAURETANIA, 1939-1965

Twin screw steamer. Built and completed in 1939 by Cammell Laird & Co., Birkenhead. Tonnage: 35,739 g.r.t., 20,170 net. 771.8′ x 89.3′ x 57.8′. Service speed 23 knots. Passengers: 486 cabin class, 390 tourist class and 502 third class. 780 crew. Photographed prior to her launch on 28th July 1938.

SOUVENIR COVER OF MAURETANIA'S MAIDEN VOYAGE
(Liverpool to New York: 17th June 1939)

R.M.S. MAURETANIA

MAURETANIA, 1939-1965

At the beginning of the Second World War, and after only completing four voyages across the Atlantic, the *Mauretania* was requisitioned in March 1940 and proceeded to Australia to be converted to a troop ship. At the end of the war, she had travelled more than half a million miles and carried 350,000 service personnel. Converted and refurbished at Cammell Laird's yard, Birkenhead and returning to Cunard service in 1947. Resumed transatlantic services from Southampton, Le Havre, Cork to New York, with cruising from New York during the winter.

Cunard Mauretania

MAURETANIA, 1939-1965

In 1957 the *Mauretania* was fitted with air conditioning and in 1962, her hull was painted light green for cruises sailing from New York to the Mediterranean. After three years and facing financial problems, Cunard withdrew the *Mauretania* from service on 10th November 1965. Sold the same year to Thomas Ward & Co. for scrapping at Inverkeithing, Firth of Forth.

QUEEN ELIZABETH, 1940-1968

Consort to the *Queen Mary.* Laid down at John Brown & Co, Glasgow in 1936. Launched by H.M. Queen Elizabeth on 27th September 1938. Quadruple screw steamer. Tonnage: 83,673 g.r.t; 42,011 net. 1,030' x 118.5' x 68.3'. Service Speed 29 knots. Passengers: 823 first class, 662 second class, 798 tourist class. 1,296 crew. On her completion she was the largest ship in the world and 12 feet longer than the *Queen Mary.*

R.M.S. QUEEN ELIZABETH.

QUEEN ELIZABETH, 1940-1968

On 27th February, 1940, and after a hurried completion, the *Queen Elizabeth* left the Clyde in secret for New York and safety. Her furnishings were put in store and she was converted to a troop ship. During the war, the *Queen Elizabeth* carried a total of 811,324 personnel and steamed half a million miles: in total the two Queens carried 1,243,538 personnel. Both ships played a vital part during the Second World War and the Cunard chairman, Sir Percy Bates, estimated that they probably helped to shorten the war by a year. They became the ultimate prize for U-boat captains, but their superior speed was their greatest asset and they survived the war. After the war, the *Queen Elizabeth* finally made her maiden voyage in October 1946 from Southampton to New York. 1955 — fitted with stabalisers. When she was sold in 1968, the *Queen Elizabeth* had steamed 3,470,000 miles and carried over 2.3 million passengers and service personnel.

CUNARD WHITE STAR LINER "QUEEN ELIZABETH"
WORLD'S LARGEST AND FASTEST LINER
TOURIST LOUNGE

83,673 Tons

QUEEN ELIZABETH, 1940-1968

The *Queen Elizabeth's* final voyage commenced on 29th November 1968. She had been purchased by a consortium of Philadelphia business men as a tourist attraction in Port Everglades, Florida. When this project failed, she was auctioned and purchased for £1,333,000 by C.Y. Tung of Orient Overseas Line. Renamed *Seawise University* and sailed to Hong Kong for conversion to a floating university. In January 1972 during the last stages of her conversion, serious fires started on board, lasting for three days and completely destroying the ship, which capsized and was totally written off by her owners.

R.M.S. "PARTHIA"   CUNARD WHITE STAR

PARTHIA, 1948-1961

Twin screw steamer. Sister ship to the *Media*. Built by Harland and Wolff, Belfast and completed in 1948. Tonnage: 13,362 g.r.t, 7,393 net. 531' x 70.3' x 46'. Service speed 17 knots. Passengers: 251 first class, 184 crew. Served on the Liverpool to New York route and designed to carry both passengers and 7,000 tons of cargo. Cunard's first post-war passenger ship along with the *Media*. Sold in November 1961 to the New Zealand Shipping Co. and renamed *Remuera*. Sold in 1965 to the Eastern and Australian Steam Co. and renamed *Aramac*. 1967 — Registered under the ownership of the Federal S.N. Co. and finally sold to Chen Ho Fa Steel and Iron Co., Taiwan in the same year for scrapping in Kaohsiung.

CARONIA, 1948-1968

Twin screw steamer. Cunard-White Star's first purpose-built cruise ship. Built by John Brown & Co., Clydebank, launched by Princess Elizabeth on 30th October 1947, and completed in 1948. Tonnage: 34,274 g.r.t, 7,921 net. 715' o.a., 666' b.p. x 91.5' x 65.2'. Service speed 22 knots. Passengers: 580 first class and 350 cabin class. 600 crew. Her maiden voyage commenced on 4th January 1949 from Southampton to New York. Named the "Green Goddess" because of her hull painted in three shades of green. Her immense single funnel, 53' x 46', weighed 125 tons. During her career the *Caronia* cruised all over the world, but due to Cunard's financial problems she was sold in 1968 to the Star Shipping Co., Panama and renamed *Columbia,* later renamed *Caribia* by Universal Cruise Lines. Laid up in 1970 following an engine room explosion and a fire. Sold to ship-breakers in Taiwan for $3 million in 1974 and during her final journey, she ran aground at Apra, Guam in the Pacific and broke into three sections.

Cunard R.M.S. Saxonia

SAXONIA, 1954-1963

Twin screw steamer. Built in 1954 by John Brown & Co., Clydebank. Tonnage: 21,637 g.r.t, 11,721 net. 570′ x 80′ x 46.3′. Service speed 20 knots. Passengers: 125 first class, 800 tourist class. 457 crew. The first of four new Cunarders built for the Liverpool to Canada service. Her maiden voyage commenced on 2nd September 1954, completing the journey two days faster than previous voyage times. Her cargo-carrying facility proved unworkable and in 1962, the *Saxonia* had a major refit converting her to a cruise liner and painted with a light green hull. Renamed *Carmania* in 1963.

CARMANIA, 1963-1973

The *Carmania*'s new role as a cruise ship altered her accommodation to take 117 first-class and 764 tourist-class passengers. She commenced cruising in 1963 from New York to the West Indies, and from 1964 to 1970, she also cruised in the Mediterranean. In January 1969, she went aground off the Bahamas but was only slightly damaged. The *Carmania* had a further refit in 1971 and then provided cruises from Southampton to the Canaries and the Mediterranean. Rising costs forced Cunard to withdraw the *Carmania* from regular services in 1971 and she was sold two years later to the Russian States Lines and renamed *Leonid Sobinov*.

CUNARD "CARMANIA"
22,592 TONS

POST CARD

NEPTUNE CRUISE

October 6th - 25th, 1967

FOR THE ADDRESS ONLY   POSTAGE

The beautiful 22,600-ton s.s. **Carmania**, re-nowned for its comfort, luxury, excellent service and superb cuisine, will visit North Africa, Egypt, Greece, Sicily and Portugal, with shore excursions at **Tripoli** (Leptis Magna, Sabratha), **Alexandria** (Cairo, the Pyramids), **Mykonos** and **Delos, Piraeus** (Athens, Delphi, Cape Sounion), **Palermo** (Monreale, Segesta, Cefalu), **Lisbon** (Queluz, Sintra, Mafra, etc.)

Lectures *(in aid of the Enterprise Neptune Fund).*, by Sir Trenchard Cox, C.B.E.—*late Director the Victoria & Albert Museum*, Lord Kinross—*well-known author & broadcaster.* Lady Brogan, M.A., F.S.A.—*an authority on the Roman cities of North Africa.* Lt. Gen. Sir Brian Horrocks, K.C.B., D.S.O., M.C. Mr. Denys Haynes—*keeper of Greek & Roman Antiquities, the British Museum.*

Please send information

Name ....
(BLOCK CAPITALS)

Address ....

....

PRINTED IN ENGLAND

Enterprise Neptune,

The National Trust,

42-44 Queen Anne's Gate,

London, S.W.1.

CARMANIA, 1963-1973

Between 6th-25th October, 1967, the *Carmania* was used for a historical interest cruise and to publicise the launch of 'Enterprise Neptune' organised by the National Trust. The above postcard gives details of the ports of call and the distinguished speakers who were present during the voyage.

IVERNIA, 1955-1973

Twin screw steamer. Sister ship to *Saxonia* (page 96). Built by John Brown & Co., Clydebank, launched on 14th December 1954 by the wife of the Canadian Prime Minister, and completed in June 1955. Tonnage: 21,717 g.r.t, 11,721 net. 608′ x 80′ x 46′. Service speed 20 knots. Passengers: 113 first class, 731 tourist class. 456 crew. Her maiden voyage commenced on 1st July 1955 from Greenock to Quebec and Montreal. Thereafter sailings were from Liverpool. 1957 — Southampton, Le Havre to Canada service. 1962 — Major refit to convert her to a cruise ship and renamed *Franconia.* She also suffered from Cunard's financial problems and was withdrawn from service in 1971. Sold to Russian owners in 1973 and renamed *Fedor Shalyapin.*

CUNARD R.M.S. "CARINTHIA"

CARINTHIA, 1956-1968

Twin screw steamer. Sister ship to *Sylvania*. Built by John Brown & Co., launched by Princess Margaret, and completed in 1956. Tonnage: 21,947 g.r.t, 11,630 net. 608′ x 80′ x 46′. Service speed 20 knots. Passengers: 174 first class, 682 tourist class. 461 crew. Fitted with stabilisers and air conditioning. Her maiden voyage commenced on 27th June 1956 from Liverpool and Greenock to Quebec and Montreal. Remained on this service until 1966 with voyages in the winter terminating at Halifax, Nova Scotia, due to the St. Lawrence river being blocked by ice. Sold to the Fairland Shipping Company in 1968 and renamed *Fairland*. Laid up in Southampton for the next two years. 1971 — Renamed *Fairsea* and converted in Trieste for services to Australia. 1988 — Renamed *Fair Princess*. In service.

Canard R.M.S. Sylvania

SYLVANIA, 1956-1968

Twin screw steamer. The last of the four Cunarders built for the Canadian service. Built by John Brown & Co., Clydebank and completed in 1956. Similar specifications to her sister ships except her tonnage was 22,017 g.r.t., 11,679 net. Her maiden voyage commenced in June 1957 from Greenock to Quebec and Montreal. Remained on this service until 1961, and then followed by servicing the route from Liverpool to New York with some Mediterranean cruises. After her last voyage in December 1967, she was sold in 1968 to the Sitmar Line of Genoa. Laid up with the *Carinthia* in Southampton for two years. 1970 — Converted in Italy for cruising and renamed *Fairwind*. 1988 — Renamed *Dawn Princess*. In service.

QUEEN ELIZABETH 2, 1969-

To replace the *Queen Mary* and the *Queen Elizabeth,* Cunard planned and designed the Q4; a prestigious passenger liner catering exclusively for the transatlantic and luxury cruise markets. After Cunard had secured financial loans from the Government, a consortium of British bankers and also mortgaging 11 ships, the Q4 (no.736) was laid down at John Brown's shipyard, Clydebank (later to become Upper Clyde Shipbuilders) in July 1965. Designed by Dan Wallace and Tom Kameen, one of the Q4's many features would be that it would be built smaller than the ageing *Queens* and capable of passing through both the Suez and Panama Canals. The final cost of the ship amounted to £29,091,000. Specifications: Twin screw steamer. Tonnage: 65,863 g.r.t., 37,218 net. 963′ o.a. x 105.1′ x 56′. Steam turbines.110,000 s.h.p.. 2 bow thrusters. 2 sets of stabilisers. Service speed 28 knots. 1900 passengers.

SOUVENIR COVER

Commemorating the departure
of R.M.S. Queen Elizabeth 2, on 2nd May 1969
for her Maiden Voyage from Southampton
to New York.

Cover Number 104
of a series of 500 only.

5d

RMS Queen Elizabeth 2

DEPARTURE
£1
2 MAY 69
MAIDEN
VOYAGE
SOUTHAMPTON

QUEEN ELIZABETH 2, 1969-

The Q4 was launched by Her Majesty Queen Elizabeth II on 20th September 1967 and named *Queen Elizabeth 2*: the name had been kept secret until the last minute — known only by four people including the Queen and the chairman of Cunard. The interior design of the ship during her fitting out was supervised by James Gardner and Dennis Lennon who ensured the best designs were made available for Cunard. During her trials in December 1968, serious problems were encountered with the *QE2*'s turbines and Cunard refused delivery until they had been corrected. Returned to Southampton for repairs and after further trials the *QE2* was finally handed over to Cunard on 18th April 1969. Her maiden voyage commenced on 2nd May 1969 from Southampton to New York. After her maiden voyage the *QE2* served on regular transatlantic crossings with cruising during the winter months.

103

QUEEN ELIZABETH 2, 1969-

The *QE2* has many extraordinary statistics including: 13 decks; 1,350 port holes; 557 windows; 25 miles of carpet; 64,000 items of crockery: 51,000 items of glassware; and 1,300 telephones. The ship is also capable of producing 1,000 tonnes of fresh water each day.

QUEEN ELIZABETH 2, 1969-

On 9th January, 1971, the *QE2* rescued 635 passengers and crew from the French cruise ship *Antilles*. During 1971 Cunard was sold to Trafalgar House Investments. This event resulted in speculation about the *QE2*'s future, but she remained in service. In May 1972, the ship was subjected to a bomb hoax while in mid-Atlantic for a ransom of $350,000. Four bomb-disposal experts were parachuted into the sea close to the liner. After their arrival on board, eighteen minutes before the bomb was due to go off, a thorough search was made and no bombs were found. A few months later, the hoaxer was captured in New York and jailed for twenty years.

The *QE2* had a major refit in 1972 in Southampton which resulted in the installation of luxury penthouses and her passenger accommodation altered to 604 first class and 1,223 tourist class, or 1,740 for cruising only. Her first world cruise commenced on 4th January 1975 and this annual event has continued to the present day.

In addition to the bomb hoax, many dramatic events occurred during the Seventies including extensive security arrangements during two cruises to Israel in 1973, and following an accident when oil infiltrated the boiler water in April 1974, 1,630 passengers were transferred to the Norwegian ship *Sea Venture* and taken to Bermuda to be flown home.

Further refits followed in 1976 and 1979 with her accommodation increased to 1,820 passengers. At the outbreak of the Falklands War in April 1982, the *QE2* was requisitioned by the Government and converted to a troop ship in only eight days in Southampton. All surplus fittings were removed and two heli-pads and satellite receiving equipment were fitted. On Wednesday, 12th May 1982 the *QE2*, under the command of Capt. Peter Jackson, set sail with the Fifth Brigade — the Scots and Welsh Guards and the Gurkhas. The *QE2* refuelled at Freetown and stopped at Ascension Island for supplies, finally arriving at South Georgia. After her arrival troops were transferred to various ships including the *Canberra*, the *Norland* and H.M.S. *Antrim*. The *QE2* then took on 640 survivors from HMS *Coventry, Antelope* and *Ardent*. With adverse weather conditions approaching, the *QE2* departed South Georgia on 28th May and after steaming 14,967 miles in total, the *QE2* arrived back in Southampton on Friday, 11th June to a welcome from Her Majesty The Queen Mother and many thousands of people.

QUEEN ELIZABETH 2, 1969-

Following her service as a troop ship, the *QE2* was refurbished back to her usual luxury appearance with the notable change of her hull being painted grey. The refit in Southampton took nine weeks and was completed on 14th August. The new hull colour proved impractical and shortly after her refit she was repainted with a black hull. In October 1985 a contract was signed for a major refit which included the *QE2* to be converted from steam to diesel-electric propulsion. A year later in October, the *QE2* arrived in Bremerhaven and the extensive work costing £92 million and 1,700,000 man-hours was finally completed after successful trials on 25th April 1987. Further 'teething-troubles' continued after the refit and new propellers were fitted in July 1988. Today, the *QE2* remains the flagship of the Cunard fleet and continues to give unrivalled service to the company; undoubtedly the finest ship in the world.

CUNARD ADVENTURER, 1971-1977

Twin screw motor ship. Built by Rotterdamsche Droogdok Maats Co., Holland for Overseas National Airways and completed in 1971. Purchased by Cunard on the stocks in July 1970. Tonnage: 14,151 g.r.t. 484' x 72'. Service speed 20kts. Passengers: 740 one class. 300 crew. Her maiden voyage commenced on 9th October 1971 from Southampton to the Mediterranean ports including Tangier and Naples. Serviced American cruises to the West Indies from the east coast of America. Sold on 1st March 1977 to Klosters Rederi, Oslo and renamed *Sunward II*.

CUNARD AMBASSADOR, 1972-1974

Twin screw motor ship. Built by P. Smit, jr, Rotterdam. Sister ship to *Cunard Adventurer* and also purchased by Cunard in July 1970. Similar specifications to her sister ship and completed in October 1972. Following an engine room fire in September 1974, the ship was declared a total loss. Fortunately, there were no passengers on board and no crew were injured.
Sold to C. Clausen of Copenhagen and renamed *Linda Clausen*. Converted to a livestock carrier for service between Australia and the Persian Gulf. 1980 — Sold to Panamanian owners and renamed *Procyon*. 1983 — Sold to Qatar Transport and Marine Services, Doha. Following an engine room fire in July of the same year, she was scrapped in Kaohsiung in September 1984.

CUNARD COUNTESS, 1976-

Built by Burmeister and Wain, Copenhagen and launched in September 1974. Fitted out by Industrie Navali Meccanini, La Spezia, Italy and completed in 1976. Tonnage: 17,586 g.r.t.. 534' x 74'. Service speed 19kts. 950 passengers. 400 crew. Based in San Juan, Puerto Rico for cruises in the West Indies. Served as a troopship between Ascension and Port Stanley in 1982. Reconverted to a cruise liner by Malta Dry Dock Co. in May 1983.

CUNARD PRINCESS, 1977-

Built by B. & W., Copenhagen as the *Cunard Conquest*. Fitted out by I.N.M.A., La Spezia, renamed *Cunard Princess* in 1976, and completed in 1977. Sister ship to *Cunard Countess* with similar specifications. Based in New York and used for cruises to the West Indies. Chartered in 1980 by Lauro Lines for Mediterranean cruising and during the 1980s, she cruised off the west coast of America to Alaska — based in Vancouver — and during winter months, she cruised to Mexico — based in Los Angeles. Both ships remain two of the world's most luxurious cruise ships.

SAGAFJORD, 1983-

Motor ship. Built by Societe des Forges et Chantiers de la Mediterranee, La Seyne sur Mer, France and launched on 13th June 1964. Tonnage: 24,109 g.r.t.. 620' x 82'. Service speed 20 knots. 507 passengers. Entered service for Norwegian American Cruises (N.A.C.) in 1965. In 1980 the *Sagafjord* was given a £12 million refit at the Blohm and Voss shipyard, Hamburg. The refit included the installation of 15 de-luxe cabins and an air conditioning system. Purchased along with her sister ship, the *Vistafjord,* by Cunard in May 1983. Awarded a five-star rating as a cruise liner in 1984.

VISTAFJORD, 1983-
Motor ship. Built by Swan Hunter Shipbuilders Ltd., Newcastle-upon-Tyne and launched on 15th
May 1972. Tonnage: 24,492 g.r.t.. 629' x 82'. Service speed 20 kts. 736 passengers. 390 crew.
Her maiden voyage in 1973 was from Oslo to New York. Purchased by Cunard in 1983. A five-star
rated cruise ship.